D0197977

ALASKA'S
BIRDS

— A GUIDE TO SELECTED SPECIES —

ALASKA NORTHWEST BOOKS™
Anchorage • Seattle • Portland

Acknowledgments

*Many people helped me by providing information through interviews, sending
publications, or editing the manuscript and selected articles. I specially thank
Brad Andras, Richard Carstensen, Dan Gibson, Richard Gordon, Jim King,
Vivian Mendenhall, Chuck O'Clair, Rita O'Clair, Mark Schwan, Dave
Sonneborn, Art Sowls, Gus van Vliet, and Mary Willson.*

Copyright © 1994 by Robert H. Armstrong

All rights reserved. No part of this book may be reproduced or transmitted in
any form or by any means, electronic or mechanical, including photocopying,
recording, or by any information storage and retrieval system, without written
permission of Alaska Northwest Books™.

Library of Congress Cataloging-in-Publication Data
Armstrong, Robert H., 1936-
    Alaska's birds : a guide to selected species / by Robert H.
Armstrong.
       p.   cm.
      Includes bibliographical references (pp. 96 and 118) and index.
      ISBN 0-88240-455-5 (acid-free paper)
      1. Birds—Alaska   I. Title.
QL684.A4A73 1994
598.29798—dc20   93-51034
                                             CIP

Managing Editor: Ellen Harkins Wheat
Editor: Lorna Price
Designer: Elizabeth Watson
Illustrations: Jim Hays
Maps: Vikki Lieb

All photos are by the author except the following: ANIMALS/ANIMALS,
A. G. Nelson: p. 61; VIREO, R. and N. Bowers: 22, 25, 29, 56; H. Clarke: 86;
Rob Curtis: 81; C. H. Greenewalt: 82; B. Henry: 94, 118; S. J. Lang: 60, 120:
A. and E. Morris: 31; R. L. Pitman: 23; D. Roby/K. Brink: 32, 34, 38, 51; R.
Shallenberger: 20; P. La Tourrette: 67.

PHOTOS. *Front cover:* Arctic Tern at nest, with Mendenhall Glacier in back-
ground, Juneau. *Back cover:* Trumpeter Swan. Photo by VIREO, R. and N.
Bowers. *Title Page:* Rufous Hummingbird feeding on blueberry nectar.

The map on p. 9 is adapted from the U.S. Fish and Wildlife brochure
2410-2079, *To Have and To Hold: Alaska's Migratory Birds.* Washington, D.C.:
Government Printing Office, 1971.

Alaska Northwest Books™
An imprint of Graphic Arts Center Publishing Co.
Editorial office: 2208 NW Market Street, Suite 300, Seattle, WA 98107
Catalog and order dept.: P.O. Box 10306, Portland, OR 97210
  800-452-3032

Printed on acid-free paper in the United States of America

— CONTENTS —

Discovering Alaska's Birds 6
Families and Selected Species 14

Alaska's Biogeographic Regions

from Kessel and Gibson, 1978

SIBERIA

Barrow

NORTHERN

Chukchi Sea

B R O O K

K

A L

Bering Strait

WESTERN

Seward Peninsula

Nome

CENTRA

Saint Lawrence *Island*

Gambell

ALASKA MARITIME NWR

Yukon River

A L A S K

McK

Bering

YUKON DELTA NATIONAL WILDLIFE REFUGE

DEN
NATIO
PAR
PRES

ALASKA MARITIME NWR

Nunivak Island

Kuskokwim River

Sea

K
N

Ho

K
Penin

St. Paul Island

Pribilof Islands

St. George Island

SOUTHWESTERN

Koc

Kodiak Island

Cold Bay

Alaska Peninsula

Izembek Bay

IZEMBEK NWR

ALASKA MARITIME NATIONAL WILDLIFE REFUGE

ALASKA MARITIME NATIONAL WILDLIFE REFUGE

Attu Islan

SEE INSET

Pacific Ocean

Arctic Ocean

Beaufort Sea

ARCTIC NATIONAL
WILDLIFE REFUGE

R A N G E

K A

t Yukon

Porcupine River

Yukon

UKON FLATS
NATIONAL
DLIFE REFUGE

River

CANADA

USA

HIGHWAY

Chena Hot Springs
rbanks
Chena River
State Rec. Area

ALASKA

R A N G E

DENALI HWY

RICHARDSON HWY

Wrangell Mountains

N

W   E

S

NWR = NATIONAL WILDLIFE REFUGE

0   miles   100

0   km   100

YUKON

TERRITORY

St. Elias Range

BRITISH

COLUMBIA

nchorage
ter Marsh

Cordova

ward

Copper R. Delta

Prince William Sound

ALASKA MARITIME NWR

aiswell Islands

OUTHCOASTAL

Stikine R.

Haines

Juneau

GLACIER BAY NATIONAL
PARK & PRESERVE

Gustavus

SOUTHEASTERN

Saint Lazaria Islands

Sitka

Petersburg

Wrangell

Gulf Of Alaska

ALASKA
MARITIME
NWR

Craig

Ketchikan

Prince of Wales Island

l e u t i a n   I s l a n d s

ASKA   MARITIME   NATIONAL   WILDLIFE   REFUGE

DISCOVERING
ALASKA'S BIRDS

Bald Eagle

Alaska plays an important, even essential role in the lives of birds found throughout the world. The state provides nesting and feeding habitats for hundreds of full-time and part-time bird residents. This pocket guide is designed to introduce you to the importance of the Far North to birds, where to find and photograph them, how to learn more about them, and how they are linked to habitats around the world. It presents the most interesting information I could find about Alaska's birds through interviews with experts, personal experiences, and written reports.

Short essays cover each bird family (except those with only rare birds) occurring in Alaska and selected species within them. Species included here were chosen for four reasons, in order of importance: birds of North America found only in Alaska, and/or those adapted especially for life in the north—the Emperor Goose and Willow Ptarmigan, for example; birds that visitors to Alaska most often look for, such as the Bald Eagle or the Horned Puffin; birds with interesting and unusual habits, like the American Dipper and Red-breasted Sapsucker; and finally, a few species that complete the family coverage, which accounts for the Warbling Vireo and the European Starling, for example.

Alaska's vastness makes it difficult for visitors to know where to look for birds. One chapter covers many of Alaska's more accessible birding "hot spots." It also lists bird-finding guides and checklists of birds for specific areas of the state. The chapter on photographing birds discusses techniques that have proved useful to me during 30 years in the field and may help make your birding trip in Alaska a photographic success.

The photographs, illustrations, and remarks about plumage and habits will help you identify the selected species. I have avoided overlap with *Guide to the Birds of Alaska*, my other book, which covers identification of Alaska's birds in more detail as well as their status, distribution, and habitat. And so the two books complement each other.

Here, as elsewhere in the world, the health and vigor of bird populations reveal the condition of the habitats on which they depend for nesting and food. As we become aware of these interdependencies, we also come to understand their significance for the health and well-being of our own species, and the importance of protecting birds and their habitats, not only in Alaska but everywhere.

ALASKA, A SPECIAL PLACE FOR BIRDS

As of December 31, 1993, 443 species of birds have been identified in Alaska (based on D. D. Gibson's 1993 *Checklist of Alaska Birds*). Of these species, 148 are either considered accidentals, with only one or very few records, or birds that occur here at irregular intervals in very small numbers. Thus about 295 bird species occur in Alaska on a regular annual basis. Roughly 100 are year-round residents, while about 200 others, the migrants, come to the state only at certain times of the year for nesting and/or feeding.

Resident Birds

Many of the species that remain year-round in Alaska must adapt during the long winter to feed on fewer or different food items from their summer diet. Their winter foraging needs are further complicated by greatly reduced daylight in the Far North, less available habitat because of ice and snow cover, and the need to keep warm.

Blue Grouse, for example, switch from a summer diet of succulent plants, seeds, berries, and insects to winter fare of buds and the fibrous needles of Sitka spruce trees. In winter, ptarmigan eat mostly willow twigs and buds. The digestive tracts of both of these species contain special bacteria that aid in the digestion of this tough material. Grouse and ptarmigan also have a crop—a food storage organ that can be filled while the birds are active during the short winter day, and then its contents can be digested later, allowing them to keep their metabolism and body temperature elevated at night. Redpolls have an enlarged esophagus that acts like a crop, and they typically eat large amounts of food just before roosting for the night.

Ptarmigan, Ruffed Grouse, and Snow Buntings may survive bitter winter storms and nights by plunging into and under the snow, where the temperature may be many degrees warmer than at the surface. Many birds conserve body heat by roosting together; chickadees, for example, may pack themselves together in holes in tree trunks.

A number of resident birds are water birds and are found wherever open water exists, from spring-fed streams in the Interior to open leads in the sea ice to the coastal waters of the south coast.

Many northern-adapted bird species develop extra fat, more feathers, and a higher resting metabolic rate. Yet as we sit cozy and warm in our heated homes during a raging Alaskan winter storm, we can only marvel at the endurance and survival of birds that spend the winter with us, even though they have these and other adaptations.

Migrant Birds

Millions of birds migrate from all continents and many islands of the world to nest in Alaska. Wheatears and

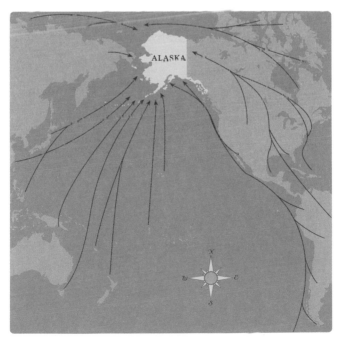

Yellow Wagtails fly all the way from Africa, while Arctic Warblers come from the Philippines. Bristle-thighed Curlews, which nest only in Alaska, come from Hawaii and the Central Pacific islands. Golden-plovers migrate from a variety of places including Hawaii, India, Australia, Tasmania, New Zealand, and the southern tip of South America. Other shorebirds such as White-rumped and Baird's Sandpipers, Greater Yellowlegs, turnstones, Red Knots, and Sanderlings travel from South America—some from as far south as Patagonia, a distance of over 8,000 miles. The Arctic Tern migrates the farthest distance of any bird to nest in Alaska, all the way from the waters of the Antarctic—up to 10,000 miles. Many waterfowl come to nest in Alaska from their wintering areas throughout the United States, Canada, and Mexico.

Some birds nest elsewhere but fly to Alaska to feed. The Sooty and Short-tailed Shearwaters nest on islands in the Southern Hemisphere during our winter, and then migrate in the millions to feed in summer off the coast of Alaska, in the Bering Sea and North Pacific. The Black-footed Albatross travels to feed in the Gulf of Alaska after nesting on the northwestern Hawaiian Islands and else-where. Snow Geese from Siberia feed on the Yukon River Delta, and Snow Geese from Canada forage for food on the Arctic National Wildlife Refuge. The entire Canadian and Siberian populations of Brant feed for a month at Izembek Bay before heading south for the winter.

Habitat

Alaska has a great diversity of bird habitat. Most of its land, so important to nesting and feeding birds, is still eco-logically undisturbed by humans. The most extensive tracts of virgin old-growth trees left in the United States can be found within the 16.8-million-acre Tongass National Forest in southeastern Alaska; here nest more Bald Eagles and Marbled Murrelets than anywhere else in North America. Both species choose these old-growth trees for nesting sites.

Alaska's coast is dotted with small, remote islands that provide excellent nesting habitat for colonial nesting seabirds. Biologists estimate that 50 million seabirds nest each year in the state. The entire North American populations of some ·

species nest here: Kittlitz's Murrelet, Crested Auklet, Whiskered Auklet, Parakeet Auklet, Aleutian Tern, Red-legged Kittiwake, and Red-faced Cormorant nest here. Most of the North American populations of several other species, among them Tufted and Horned Puffins, also nest in Alaskan territory. In addition, the food-rich waters of the North Pacific and Bering Sea attract an additional 35 to 85 million seabirds (which go elsewhere to nest) each summer.

Alaska has between 170 and 233 million acres of wetlands, roughly 70 percent of the nation's total, which are so important to waterfowl, shorebirds, and other species dependent on this habitat for food and nesting. For example, the Yukon-Kuskokwim Delta, an immense, roadless, water-rich area in western Alaska, hosts millions of birds each year, including about 90 percent of the world's population of Emperor Geese and all of the cackling Canada Geese. Most Greater White-fronted Geese, Black Turnstones, Western Sandpipers, and Tundra Swans found in the Pacific nest within this delta. Located much farther upstream, in east-central Alaska, the Yukon Flats National Wildlife Refuge, mostly wetlands, includes more than 40,000 lakes, ponds, and sloughs. These flats have one of the highest densities of nesting ducks on the North American continent, contributing more than 2 million ducks to the nation each year. The Copper River Delta in southcentral Alaska is the greatest natural delta left in temperate North America and has the largest contiguous wetland on the Pacific Coast of North America. Considered crucial to migrating shorebirds from all over the world, this wetland serves as many as 20 million shorebirds that stop to rest, feed, and refuel here each spring before heading to their breeding grounds in western and northern Alaska, Siberia, and Canada.

These are only a few examples. Scattered throughout Alaska are numerous national wildlife refuges, national parks, monuments and preserves, wilderness areas, wild rivers, conservation areas, state critical habitat areas, marine parks, game refuges and sanctuaries, recreation areas, and parks. Each area has its own unique habitat and value for Alaska's birds, and the habitat protection these land classifications offer will help ensure our birds' future.

Despite this habitat protection, however, Alaska's birds

are still quite vulnerable. The *Exxon Valdez* oil spill in 1989 took the lives of an estimated 300,000 to 645,000 birds, the highest death toll of birdlife ever documented from an oil spill. The high concentration of specific bird species nesting or feeding in certain areas of the state makes them even more vulnerable to human-caused disasters such as oil spills.

Furthermore, Alaska has not been all that considerate of its birds in other ways. Old-growth forests have been lost to clear-cut logging and urban development. Wetlands have been eliminated near our cities to make way for expanding airports and shopping centers. Ground-nesting birds on many of Alaska's treeless coastal islands have been devastated by foxes released by fur farmers, by rats escaped from shipwrecks, or by descendants of rats that arrived with the military during World War II. The range of some species of waterfowl has been greatly reduced by summer hunting. And Alaska's gill-net fisheries kill thousands of aquatic diving birds each year. In addition, the drift-net and long-line fisheries of other countries operating in the North Pacific are killing hundreds of thousands of birds each year, many of which would be of Alaskan origin. For instance, an estimated 9 percent of the Tufted Puffins breeding in the Aleutians are killed annually in these fisheries. The dumping of garbage, especially plastics, and discarded fishing gear into the ocean kills Alaska's birds through their ingestion of the debris and their entanglement in it.

Because about two-thirds of Alaska's birds migrate here from elsewhere, they are also dependent on habitat outside Alaska—where they winter as well as where they stop to rest, feed, and refuel while en route to the state.

An alarming loss of wetlands has occurred outside of Alaska, where many of Alaska's migrating waterfowl and shorebirds winter and feed. Over 50 percent loss has been estimated for the Lower 48 states. In California alone, where a major portion of Alaska's nesting waterfowl spend the winter, 91 percent of wetlands has already been lost to development and agriculture. Wetland loss in the United States, excluding Alaska, continues at an estimated rate of 350,000 to 500,000 acres each year. In his excellent book *Tracks in the Sky*, Peter Steinhart writes about the loss of wetlands along the Pacific flyway: "We are slowly strangling

12

the flyway. One day, we may look out over an endless plain of concrete and asphalt and glass and find that we have drained the skies."

The loss of tropical forests in South America affects the wintering habitat of Alaska's Western Wood-Pewee, Gray-cheeked Thrush, Swainson's Thrush, Townsend's Warbler, Blackpoll Warbler, and Northern Waterthrush. Tourism in Hawaii is considered a threat to the maintenance of Bristle-thighed Curlews, which nest only in Alaska. The Platte and North Platte rivers in central Nebraska are in danger of losing the essential habitat on which over 90 percent of Alaska's and the world's population of Sandhill Cranes stops to feed, rest, and refuel every year.

Throughout the world, the loss of habitat for Alaska's birds continues. On the other hand, what we do in Alaska will affect the birds that others enjoy on their wintering grounds elsewhere. "Alaska's birds" are, in fact, a global concern.

FAMILIES AND
SELECTED
SPECIES

Black-billed Magpie

~ LOONS ~

All species of loons found worldwide are also found in Alaska. Loons are truly birds of the North; only the Common Loon breeds south of Canada. The loon's voice, like the wolf's howl or the sight of a grizzly bear, gives us a sense of the wild. Their eerie call establishes a pair bond between breeding adults and declares and helps them hold their territories—usually an entire lake or pond. Common and Yellow-billed Loons give a variety of very loud laughing, yodeling, and wailing wolflike calls. The calls of the other loon species, just as dramatic, may include quacks, growls, croaks, shrieks, squeals, yelps, ascending whistles, wailing sirens, and piercing screams. The wildness of their calls seems to fit the wild places loons choose to nest—they favor lakes and ponds well away from human disturbance.

Members of the Loon family have a number of adaptations for swimming underwater after fish. These characteristics include a streamlined appearance because of their relatively long, sharply pointed bill and webbed feet set far back on the body. They have many solid bones, which makes them less buoyant; bones of most other birds contain air spaces. Loons can submerge gradually by compressing their feathers, eliminating air trapped in them, and by deflating their lungs. Their average underwater dive lasts about 1 minute, but dives of up to 3 minutes have been recorded.

Common Loon numbers in the northeastern United States have dropped dramatically since around 1960. Some states report a 35 to 75 percent decline from previous population levels. Increased powerboating frightens loons off their nests, exposing the eggs to predation. Acidification of lakes kills fish, and the young loons starve because although adults can fly to other lakes to feed, the unfledged young cannot. On their saltwater wintering grounds, thousands of loons have been killed by oil spills and mercury poisoning.

Common Loon

15

Red-throated Loon
With young. Length: 25 ½ in.

The Red-throated Loon is the most widely distributed breeding loon in Alaska and possibly the most numerous. The summer adult has a gray head, red throat, and plain brown back. It is most common along the coastal areas of the state. The Red-throated Loon enters into the life and stories of the Eskimos to a greater extent than other loon species because it is more abundant close to the river mouths and saltwater lagoons where these Natives live. After nesting, the Red-throated Loon winters at sea along the entire Pacific coast of Alaska.

For nesting and rearing their young, most loons choose a fairly large lake or pond with fish. But the Red-throated Loon usually selects small, shallow, fishless ponds. These small ponds thaw sooner in the spring, allowing this loon to begin nesting earlier. The Red-throated Loon can also become airborne within a shorter stretch of water than heavier loons; hence it can utilize smaller bodies of water for nesting. To feed, however, it must fly to larger, fish-rich lakes or to the ocean, which probably explains why most Red-throated Loons choose ponds along the coast or near larger freshwater lakes.

I once sat in a blind and watched a pair of Red-throated Loons with their young on a small pond. Twice the adults brought Pacific herring and Pacific sand lance to their young. To obtain these marine fish, the adults had to fly about 2 miles.

⸺ GREBES ⸺

Grebes are aquatic diving birds with elaborate courtship rituals. When courting they engage in "head-shaking" while facing each other, and also a mutual "penguin dance"—just two of several such antics.

I waded into a small pond near Fairbanks and set up my tripod and camera near a Horned Grebe's nest in about 2 feet of water. I wanted to trigger the camera with a remote device from about 200 feet away, so I sat watching the nest with binoculars. In a few minutes a grebe cautiously approached. At first it swam slowly around my setup—then it reared vertically out of the water and "danced" around the tripod several times, splashing water everywhere with its feet. It then swam to its nest and seemed oblivious to the clicks and whirrs of my shutter and motor drive.

Horned Grebe with young

Horned Grebe
On nest. Length: 13 ½ in.

The summer adult Horned Grebe has broad, buffy ear tufts, a black head, and a red neck. Horned Grebes are primarily carnivorous, with small fish, aquatic insects, and leeches probably making up most of their diet in Alaska. They are reported to purposely eat their feathers, which may constitute up to 55 percent of their stomach contents. Some ornithologists speculate that the feathers may protect their stomachs from the sharp fish bones that their gizzards do not adequately crush.

On their nesting grounds, Horned Grebes make bizarre sounds. Loud croaks, barks, and shrieks are not uncommon, as well as various clucking, mewing, and gurgling sounds. Horned Grebes, as do the other grebe species, carry young on their back. They may even dive and resurface with the young clinging tenaciously by grasping their parent's feathers with their beaks. These sounds and sights are a nice addition to Alaska's shallow ponds, sloughs, and lakes where these birds nest.

⏤ ALBATROSSES ⏤

Albatrosses are goose-sized seabirds that frequent the Gulf of Alaska, the North Pacific, and the southern Bering Sea. After nesting on the northwestern Hawaiian Islands and elsewhere, they visit our waters in summer and feed well away from shore on fish, squid, and waste from fishing boats.

Albatrosses were once slaughtered on their nesting grounds. The wings were used for ladies' hats, and the feathers for mattress and pillow stuffing. These feather-hunters eliminated many of the original nesting colonies of the albatross species that visit Alaska; the Short-tailed Albatross was brought almost to extinction in this manner. It is on the Endangered Species List, although once it was the most common albatross in the Aleutians. Only about 400 individuals remain alive in the world today.

Albatrosses may have the longest life span of any bird that visits Alaska. Banding of Laysan Albatrosses has shown that they commmonly live at least 40 years and often longer.

Members of this family are called "tubenoses" because their nostrils are enclosed in a tube or tubes on the top of the bill. The tubular structure also contains a valvelike pocket that may possibly help these seabirds to detect the varying pressures produced by wind blowing over water.

Short-tailed Albatross

Black-footed Albatross
Length: 32 in. Wingspan: 7 ft.

The Black-footed Albatross is dark-bodied, with dark feet and bill; older birds are white about the head. This bird follows ships, sometimes soaring nearby for hours with scarcely a wingbeat. Their long, narrow wings produce less drag than the wings of most other birds, and while following ships they can even soar into the wind by using the updrafts created by waves, much as hawks use updrafts over mountain ridges. They may also take advantage of the wind that blows much more slowly near the surface, retarded by friction from passing over the waves. To utilize these updrafts and wind gradients, the albatross may travel in a sort of zigzag pattern while following a ship.

─ FULMARS, PETRELS, SHEARWATERS ─

Fulmars, petrels, and shearwaters comprise the family Procellariidae, a name derived from the Latin word *procella*—a storm or a violent wind. Their home is the sometimes stormy open sea, and we see them mostly within the Gulf of Alaska, around the Aleutian Islands, and in the Bering Sea. Their common names also tell us something about them. The name "fulmar," from Old Norse, means "foul gull," an epithet that comes from its habit of spitting a foul-smelling liquid at intruders. The name "petrel" comes from Saint Peter and his attempt to walk on water—with its webbed feet, the bird pushes away from the water and seems to patter across the surface while dipping for food, thus appearing to walk. The shearwater's name describes its flight, often near the surface, tilting from side to side and "shearing" the water with its wings.

Although the sense of smell is poorly developed in most birds, these birds, also called "tubenoses," can find food by smell alone. Northern Fulmars and Sooty Shearwaters are attracted to the smell of fish oils, squid, and krill. Like the albatrosses these birds can soar rapidly by using the wind gradients and updrafts produced over water.

Members of this family typically regurgitate a very foul (to us), musky-smelling, but vitamin-rich oil. They feed this oil to their chicks, and also to each other during courtship. They also use it to preen and to repel intruders. While rearing their young, many tubenoses forage up to several hundred miles from their nesting site and carry the food back to their chicks by swallowing it into their own stomach. As a consequence, most of the food they feed their young consists of partially digested marine organisms mixed with the oil produced in the adult birds' stomach. The youngsters thrive on this diet and may end up weighing twice as much as their parents before they leave the nesting grounds. A heavy body is a distinct advantage to the unfledged chicks, as the adults may abandon them weeks before they are able to fly, and the young must then survive off their stored body fat.

Short-tailed Shearwater
Length: 14 in.

The Short-tailed Shearwater, one of the most abundant birds in Alaska, is truly an international species, nesting and breeding in fall in southern Australia, and feeding in summer in Alaska's food-rich waters. In summer, roughly 30 million of these birds migrate through the North Pacific, most concentrating in the Bering Sea as far north as Bering Strait. During these flights, as many as 1,000 birds per minute have been reported moving through narrow passes, for periods up to several hours long. Some make about a 20,000-mile round trip.

In Australia this shearwater is known as the mutton-bird. The young, flightless birds are commercially harvested when they weigh about two pounds. Most of the bird is utilized, including the down and feathers for bedding, and the oily stomach content for pharmaceuticals; their flesh, either fresh or pickled, is used for human food.

Short-tailed Shearwaters nest in dense colonies averaging about 1 nest per square yard. The nest is a chamber lined with dead leaves in a burrow up to 2 yards long. The birds dig them into the ground, usually under tussocks. They tend to have the same mate year after year, and return to the same burrow or to one nearby. Incubation is shared between sexes, with each shift lasting about 12 to 14 days. The adult birds visit the colony only during darkness, perhaps to minimize predation.

~ STORM-PETRELS ~

Storm-petrels are slightly smaller than a robin, and typically hover and patter with their feet across the ocean's surface in search of food.

Fork-tailed Storm-Petrel
Length: 8 ½ in.

In Alaska two species of storm-petrels occur—the Fork-tailed Storm-Petrel and Leach's Storm-Petrel. Both species feed on the open ocean and nest on offshore islands. While the larger seabirds use wind gradients and soar above the waves during windy weather, the little, fragile-appearing storm-petrels flutter about between the wave crests. Here they seek protection from the wind and take advantage of the currents and updrafts created by the waves.

Early sailors named these birds "stormy-petrels" because they typically concentrated on the more protected leeward side of the ships during heavy gales and seas. This affinity for ships probably brought the storm-petrel into the folklore of early sailors. They were considered by some to be storm prophets, their protectors, the souls of drowned sailors, but also devil-birds that flitted over the corpses of those lost at sea.

— CORMORANTS —

Rather drab-looking from a distance, during breeding season the cormorant reveals some of the most vivid colors in the avian world. The cobalt blue face, eyes, and throat of Brandt's Cormorant and the emerald green eyes and ruby red throat and face of the Pelagic Cormorant are as vivid as the colors of any tropical parrot.

Cormorants are well equipped to swim rapidly underwater after fish. Their unusually large feet have webbing between all 4 toes, unlike ducks and loons, which have webbing between only 3. Similar to loons, cormorants have solid bones and the ability to squeeze air from their plumage, allowing them to submerge more easily. Unlike ducks, their feathers are "wettable," or not entirely waterproof, which makes them even less buoyant and therefore better adapted for underwater activities. As a consequence, however, cormorants must hold their wings outstretched to dry them after swimming. A line of cormorants in this stately posture is a familiar sight along our coastal waters where these birds live.

Pelagic Cormorant drying its wings

Red-faced Cormorant
Length: 29 in.

Within North America this cormorant is found only in Alaska, where the estimated number of breeding birds is around 130,000. Elsewhere, they are found only on the Komandorskiye and Kurile islands of Russia. They can be seen on the Gull Island tour from Homer and from the ferries that venture into the Gulf of Alaska. They usually nest in colonies on the ledges of cliffs bordering the sea and sometimes on small piles of rocks and small shelves on volcanic cinder cones.

Cormorants have a gular pouch, a patch of loose skin on the upper throat that serves to hold fish larger than they can swallow. It also holds partially digested fish for the young to feed upon and helps the bird expel extra heat when it "pants," and its brilliant colors are important in courtship and territorial displays. The courting male, for example, extends his colorful gular pouch while throwing back his head in front of the female. In addition, the Red-faced Cormorant courts the female by holding nest material in his bill.

— BITTERNS, HERONS —

Great Blue Heron

Bitterns and herons are long-legged birds that stalk the shallows of lakes, marshes, and coastal waters searching for small fish, their chief food. Most species have a long neck and a rather long, straight, pointed bill.

Although 8 species of this family have been seen in Alaska, only 2, the American Bittern and the Great Blue Heron, occur here on a regular basis. The American Bittern, considered rare, is found mostly along the major mainland river systems of southeastern Alaska. The bittern is a skulker in the heavy marsh vegetation and difficult to see. We usually become aware of their presence by either flushing them into flight or by hearing their very unusual calls. Their calls, which may carry for more than one-half mile, sound somewhat like an old-fashioned pump in combination with an iron stake being hammered into the ground (*pump-er-lunk*).

Great Blue Heron
Length: 47 in.

One of the bird questions I most often hear as a resident of southeastern Alaska is: "Where do Great Blue Herons nest?" These large birds, with their 6-foot wingspan, are very obvious when feeding on the open mudflats, but their nests are well hidden; the birds are shy and very secretive.

The habits of the Great Blue Heron and the Bald Eagle are similar in some ways. Both are year-round residents in southern Alaska, both feed mostly on fish, and both build nests out of sticks placed high in coniferous trees. Bald Eagle nests are often obvious structures placed in an old-growth tree that differs in structure or size from nearby trees. In contrast, the Great Blue Heron often builds its inconspicuous nest in a dense stand of trees that may be second growth.

The Great Blue Heron nests in colonies, but the Bald Eagle makes a solitary nest. Colonial nesting could arise from social attraction as well as from a lack of the need to defend territory. Bald Eagles, however, are highly territorial. Available food and method of hunting may play a role in their territorial behavior. A Bald Eagle spends most of its time waiting patiently for a fish, alive or dead, to present itself. During the time of nesting, fish infrequently become available to Bald Eagles, so they need to maintain large territories. Great Blue Herons, on the other hand, actively search for food along shorelines where prey such as gunnels, sculpins, and flounder are available. Because their food sources are plentiful and more evenly distributed, herons may require correspondingly less territory.

— SWANS, GEESE, DUCKS —

About 10 million swans, geese, and ducks nest in Alaska each year, making the state critical habitat for North America's waterfowl. Over half the North American population of Trumpeter and Tundra Swans, Greater White-fronted Geese, Greater Scaups, and Harlequin Ducks nest in Alaska, and substantial numbers of Northern Pintails, American Wigeons, and Canvasbacks use Alaska for nesting. After nesting, waterfowl from Alaska travel to all the other American states, most Canadian provinces, Mexico, and as far south as Panama.

Alaska also feeds and protects waterfowl that nest in other countries. Snow Geese from Canada come to feed at the Arctic National Wildlife Refuge in northeastern Alaska each fall. Steller's Eiders migrate from coastal Siberia to feed and winter in Izembek Lagoon on the Alaska Peninsula. All Brants from Canada and Russia intermingle with those from Alaska and spend 6 to 9 weeks each fall on Izembek Lagoon and nearby areas around Cold Bay. They feed on eelgrass and fatten for a 3,000-mile nonstop migration, in late October or early November, across the Gulf of Alaska to California or Mexico.

Many waterfowl winter in Alaska. Huge rafts of scoters and mixed groups of goldeneyes, Buffleheads, Oldsquaws, and others are a familiar sight within the protected, ice-free bays and inlets of our marine waters. Large concentrations of eiders spend the winter around Kodiak Island, the Alaska Peninsula, the Aleutian Islands, and the ice-free parts of the Bering Sea. Most swans and geese leave Alaska for the winter; however, nearly all of the Emperor Geese that nest in Alaska and most of the Vancouver Canada Geese remain.

Most members of the waterfowl family have a bill with toothlike ridges that interlock when the bill is closed. These ridges strain water from such foods as plants, seeds, and aquatic invertebrates. The merganser's bill has sharp, sawlike edges to help it hold slippery fish.

Trumpeter Swan
Length: 65 in.

The Trumpeter Swan is the largest member of the waterfowl family. Males average 28 pounds and females 22, but some individuals may weigh as much as 40 pounds. Seeing these huge birds, with their 6- to 8-foot wingspan, migrating overhead in Vs and lines, is a spectacular event available in a few places during spring and fall. Our attention is first drawn to their loud, hornlike call, *ko-hoh*, or a variation.

In 1990 the U.S. Fish and Wildlife Service counted 13,340 Trumpeter Swans in Alaska, representing about 80 percent of the world's population. Although fewer than 100 Trumpeter Swans were thought to exist worldwide in the early 1930s, the Alaskan population at that time was probably greater, since the remoteness of their breeding grounds allowed many birds to go unnoticed. A ban on hunting them in the early 1900s and good waterfowl conservation have helped bring them back. Alaskan nesting Trumpeters have been doubling each decade since the 1950s. This has coincided with their learning to feed on most crops, grasses, and grains in the fields of southwest British Columbia and western Washington. This suggests that when the estuaries of that region were turned into harbors, the Trumpeters suffered declines and are only now recovering.

Emperor Goose
Length: 27 in.

Emperors are Alaska's most colorful goose, with their striking pattern of blue-gray scaled with black and white feathers. They have a white head, and the back of the neck is usually stained rusty from the iron deposits in the water in which they feed. Orange feet and a pink bill complete this interesting array of color.

The majority of the world's population of Emperor Geese are residents of Alaska. Nesting slightly inland along the Bering Sea, these birds are seldom far from salt water. They winter along the beaches of Kodiak Island and throughout the Aleutian Islands. They feed on a variety of forage along these beaches, including an alga called sea lettuce, and eelgrass, a type of marine flowering plant that produces long, ribbonlike leaves that float upright in the water.

The eelgrass beds of Izembek Lagoon and adjacent areas near Cold Bay are a favored feeding area for spring and fall migrating Emperor Geese.

The Emperor Goose has been declining in numbers. The population was estimated at about 150,000 in 1971 and 58,800 in 1985. The taking of eggs and adults for subsistence on their breeding grounds is thought to be the major factor in their decline.

Northern Pintail
Male. Length: 25–29 in.

Called "greyhounds of the air," pintails are sleek and slender ducks with long necks and narrow, pointed tails. Their wings are longer and narrower than those of other ducks, contributing to their elegant appearance. They are swift fliers and have been timed at speeds from 49 to 65 miles per hour.

Northern Pintails are the most abundant and widely distributed duck in Alaska, averaging over 1 million birds annually in spring and perhaps twice that by fall. Alaska becomes even more important to the North American population of pintails during years of drought in the prairie potholes of southern Canada and the northcentral United States. During such dry years, the Northern Pintail bypasses these prime breeding areas and migrates into northern Canada, Alaska, and even northeastern Siberia in search of an aquatic habitat. In one drought year, Alaska's dependable wetlands played host to about 60 percent of the pintails breeding in North America. In most years about 20 percent of the population breeds here.

Alaska's pintails also have strong ties to the state of California. Almost 85 percent of the pintails that breed in Alaska migrate to California.

Spectacled Eider
Male, female. Length: 21 in.

Most of the world's population of these birds nests in the Yukon Delta, the Arctic coastal plain of Alaska, and eastern Siberia. Where these birds spend the winter, however, is largely unknown. They are mysteriously absent from both their Alaskan and Siberian breeding grounds by September and reappear in May (in Alaska) and June (in Siberia). They are thought to winter somewhere in the Bering Sea, but no one has ever seen any large concentrations of them there.

The world's population, once thought to number between 400,000 and 500,000 birds, is also mysteriously dropping. Recent surveys of nesting Spectacled Eiders on the Yukon Delta have shown declines of over 90 percent. This is especially alarming because the Yukon Delta represents the center of its breeding range. The reasons for this decline are unknown. The U.S. Fish and Wildlife Service has recently listed the Spectacled Eider as a threatened species and appointed a recovery team of waterfowl specialists to determine what must be done to bring them back.

Harlequin Duck

Female, male. Length: 17 in.

One of Alaska's most colorful ducks, the male Harlequin is mostly slate blue with white spots and stripes and chestnut-colored flanks. The female is dusky brown, with 3 round white spots on each side of the head. Along with the American Dipper and Wandering Tattler, the Harlequin Duck has bird-breeding rights to the wildest of Alaska's streams and rivers. They usually choose the more turbulent and rock-strewn coastal and mountain streams as nesting habitat. While we frequently see them on these streams, few nests have been found in Alaska. Studies of this bird in Iceland suggest that they may often nest among the dense willow thickets so common alongside these fast-flowing streams as well as on the islands within them.

I have seen Harlequin Ducks swim underwater in streams against a swift current, lift rocks with the upper bill, then grab the dislodged aquatic insects beneath, their major food in this habitat. The birds inhabit rocky seacoasts when they are not breeding. Here they dive to feed on small crabs, limpets, chitons, periwinkles, and amphipods. Harlequin Ducks are more abundant in Alaska than elsewhere, and a visit to any of our ice-free, rocky coastal areas in winter almost guarantees a look at these unusual ducks.

Oldsquaw
Male. Length: 20 in.

The male Oldsquaw is a particularly elegant bird, with its trim diver's body and very long, pointed tail. Like the call of the loon, that of the male Oldsquaw brings wildness to mind. Echoing across the tundra, their loud, garrulous calls have been described as sounding like *ai-aidelay*, *ai-ai-aidelow*, *caloo caloo*, *ah-ahlowet*, or *ow-ow-owdle-ow*, and *alcoholic*. They call year-round, and I have often heard them while cross-country skiing near the seashore in southeastern Alaska, a thrilling sound in an otherwise quiet winter.

Oldsquaws are truly a bird of the Arctic, where they are the most numerous of the waterfowl. They breed in all of the arctic lands surrounding the North Pole, and many winter as far north as they can get, at the edge of the pack ice.

Oldsquaws dive to great depths after food and usually feed farther offshore than other diving ducks. As a consequence, they are entangled in gill nets more than any other duck. In the heyday of the Great Lakes fishery, for example, up to 27,000 Oldsquaws were reported killed by one gill net fisherman during an 8-week period!

These birds of prey have hooked beaks and sharp, curved talons for catching and holding prey. Their method of hunting varies among the species and sometimes even within a species.

Nesting Bald Eagles may spend the entire day surveying the water from high in a spruce or hemlock tree, waiting patiently for a fish to swim near the surface or float by. Other eagles may concentrate along streams and rivers to feed on dead and dying salmon. Some eagles follow river otters and steal their prey, or feed on fish injured or driven to the water's surface by feeding whales. Ospreys are also fish-eaters but have a distinct preference for live fish, which they capture by hovering and diving feet-first after them.

The Northern Harrier glides so low over the marsh that it surprises other birds before they can take wing. It has very good hearing, much better than other hawks; it hears as acutely as an owl, and can attack squeaking voles hidden by marsh vegetation without having to see them.

The small, foot-long Sharp-shinned Hawk sits concealed within the forest's foliage and dashes out to seize small birds. Concealment, quickness, and the element of surprise are its game and tactics.

The Golden Eagle, with its long wings, is expert at soaring above mountain ridges and tundra in search of ground squirrels and marmots. These birds also typically sweep the mountain ridges and slopes by flying near ground level during the subdued light of early morning or late evening, when small mammals are most active.

These predatory birds, or raptors, often break the rules we make to explain their habits. I have seen a Bald Eagle chase another bird through the forest with amazing agility. I have also seen Northern Harriers feeding on dead fish and hunting in heavy timber. While Alaska's birds of prey have evolved hunting techniques and prey preferences that minimize competition between species, most take advantage of any opportunity for a meal.

Bald Eagle

With salmon. Length: 30–43 in. Wingspan: 6 ½ –8 ft.

Unusually high numbers of Bald Eagles gather at times to feed on fish. The most notable gathering is at the Chilkat River, near Haines, where over 3,000 eagles may gather during late fall to feed on the carcasses of spawned-out chum salmon. At the Stikine River near Wrangell, 500 to 1,500 eagles gather to feed on spawning eulachon during April each year. When Pacific herring spawn, sometimes in the millions on a single beach, they often attract hundreds of eagles.

These concentrations of fish may not be available for nesting eagles. When nesting, eagles are very territorial and will not search widely for food. Instead they may be dependent on the occasional injured or dead fish floating at the water's surface. Most fish, such as salmon, herring, sculpins, or flounders, sink when they die, however, because their gas bladder collapses. A few species, mostly members of the cod and rockfish families, have a gas bladder that expands, often causing them to float when dead or injured. Studies have shown that eagles most often bring these species to their nests and young.

In winter, Bald Eagles are adept at detecting the slightest weakness in any of the larger birds that spend the winter with them. At this time they often depend on other birds for food when fish are unavailable.

— FALCONS —

Peregrine Falcon

Like hawks, falcons have hooked beaks and sharp, curved talons, but their bill is obviously toothed and notched, a characteristic absent in the hawk family. The wingtips of falcons are pointed, while those of hawks tend to be more rounded.

Most falcons plunge after their prey from above, typically power-diving (stooping) by partially folding their wings. The streamlined body shape reduces air resistance, so these birds can attain amazing speeds while plunging after prey.

Each falcon species has its foraging specialty. The small 8- to 12-inch-long American Kestrel may hunt by hovering and scanning the ground for prey, or watching from a perch. Large insects such as dragonflies as well as voles and small birds are its quarry. The slightly larger Merlin is primarily a bird-hunter, often concentrating on birds that travel in flocks over open country, such as American Pipits and Lapland Longspurs. Merlins hunt from a perch but will also fly close to the ground, remaining hidden from their prey until the last moment.

The Peregrine Falcon specializes at snatching birds from the air. It often hunts from a high cliff or tall tree and can track flying birds beyond the range of human vision. The Peregrine also employs a method called contouring, or flying low over the ground. At sea the versatile Peregrine Falcon contours behind waves to surprise marine birds.

Gyrfalcon

Gray phase. Length: 20–25 in. Wingspan: 4 ft.

Largest of all falcons, the Gyrfalcon is more uniform in color than the Peregrine Falcon and lacks its dark hood. It varies in color from mostly white to mostly black. All color variations occur in Alaska; grayish individuals are the most common.

The Gyrfalcon is a year-round resident in Alaska and may stay near its nesting area in winter if sufficient prey is available. The population of this falcon has not been severely reduced due to pesticides, unlike the more widely distributed and farther ranging Peregrine Falcon. Nevertheless, low levels of industrial pollutants have been found in some Alaskan Gyrfalcons, which they probably acquired from eating migratory birds. Even birds that spend their entire lives in a pollution-free habitat may be at risk if their prey comes from elsewhere. Gyrfalcons are not common birds anywhere. The total Alaska breeding population probably fluctuates in the neighborhood of around 500 pairs.

Ptarmigan, when available, are their major prey, and when they are the sole food, a Gyrfalcon pair needs to kill about 200 to support themselves and their brood from May to August. They are known to feed on a variety of other creatures in Alaska, including ground squirrels, voles, lemmings, Long-tailed Jaegers, alcids, waterfowl, shorebirds, gulls, songbirds, and even Short-eared Owls.

⬥ GROUSE, PTARMIGAN ⬥

Grouse and ptarmigans are chickenlike birds that forage mostly on the ground, or in trees when the ground is snow-covered.

When courting females and establishing a territory, male grouse and ptarmigan conduct elaborate rituals, and some make unusual sounds. Spruce Grouse make a whirring sound with their wings as well as a sharp cracking or snapping sound by beating their wings together in flight. Ruffed Grouse drum with their wings, which sounds like a motor starting in the distance. Male Sharp-tailed Grouse gather at dawn on a dancing-ground to circle about while drumming their feet, making rasping sounds with their tails and popping sounds with their bulging air sacs. Male Blue Grouse attract females by uttering hooting notes while sitting in a conifer. This call can be heard from a long way off and, for maximum coverage, they change the direction of hooting every few minutes. Blue Grouse males also have an area of bare skin above their eyes, called a comb, which can rapidly change color from yellow to red and back again. Male Willow Ptarmigan defend their territories by strutting and calling over a chosen section of ground and making short flights while uttering barking notes.

Grouse and ptarmigan grow "snowshoes" every fall and winter, which helps them walk on snow. Grouse grow scale-like projections along both sides of their toes, and ptarmigan develop dense feathers on both the bottom and top of each foot. In addition, before each winter the claws of ptarmigan elongate, giving them effective crampons for walking on ice.

Willow Ptarmigan in winter

Willow Ptarmigan
Male. Length: 16 in.

The male Willow Ptarmigan is the only member of this family that stays with the female while she incubates the eggs and cares for the young. He hides near the female and viciously defends her and her eggs from all intruders. While these attacks are usually aimed at gulls preying on the eggs and newborn chicks, Willow Ptarmigan have been known to attack humans and even grizzly bears. I once saw a male Willow Ptarmigan pounce on the back of a Northern Harrier and successfully drive it away. If the female is killed, the male will continue caring for the chicks.

In some areas of Alaska, and in some years, Willow Ptarmigan can be very abundant and an important food for predators. Gyrfalcons often depend on them, especially in winter, and they are an important food for others, including Rough-legged Hawks, Golden Eagles, Peregrine Falcons, Snowy Owls, and both arctic and red foxes.

The male Willow Ptarmigan molts its head and neck plumage in spring and its body plumage some months later. This gives it a distinctive two-tone look—white body and brown head and neck.

The Willow Ptarmigan has been voted the official state bird by Alaska's schoolchildren.

⏤ CRANES ⏤

Cranes are large, long-legged, long-necked wading birds. The Sandhill Crane is the only species that occurs regularly in Alaska.

Most Sandhill Cranes that nest in Alaska have wintered in Texas, New Mexico, and northern Mexico. These birds migrate to Alaska through the middle part of the Lower 48 and Canada and enter Alaska via the Tanana Valley, north of the Alaska Range. A much smaller group (20,000 to 25,000) winters in California's Central Valley and Carrizo Plain, and migrates to Alaska through the Pacific states and British Columbia.

Sandhill Crane

Sandhill Crane
Length: 34–48 in. Wingspan: 6–7 ft.

We usually first notice these cranes when they fly overhead, giving their loud, trumpetlike calls that sound somewhat like a cross between a French horn and a squeaky barn door. I have often thought that these calls sound pre-historic, and in fact this species seems to have changed little from their fossil records, which date back 9 million years.

Alaska is an important breeding ground for the world's population of Sandhill Cranes. Between 200,000 and 225,000 cranes summer in Alaska—almost half the estimated world population. Most—about two-thirds—of Alaska's breeding Sandhill Cranes nest and raise their young on the tundra flats of the Yukon-Kuskokwim Delta. The highly territorial pairs may require roughly 1 square mile in which to place their well-hidden nests.

Sandhill Cranes pair for life and periodically practice "unison calling." This loud and penetrating call is given while the male and female stand side by side or facing each other. It is done simultaneously, the female giving about 2 calls for every 1 uttered by the male. This practice is thought to reinforce existing pair bonds.

Outside of the breeding season, groups of Sandhill Cranes may "dance" with each other. This unusual behavior consists of a combination of bows, jumps, wing-flaps, and sometimes stick tosses. All ages dance. Ornithologists disagree about the function of this behavior, which may actually serve several purposes.

⸺ PLOVERS ⸺

Compared to sandpipers (p. 45), plovers have a thicker, shorter bill, shorter legs, and larger eyes. Feeding plovers typically run short distances and stop, whereas sandpipers move more continuously when feeding.

American Golden-Plover
On nest. Length: 10 in.

This bird has a golden brown back, and the male's underside is entirely black in breeding plumage. It shows a white stripe on the head, neck, and sides which extends to the breast. It winters in South America. Another species, the Pacific Golden-Plover, occurs in Alaska. In this species, the white stripe extends to the flanks. It winters in southern Asia and on islands in the central and southern Pacific Ocean. In its brown winter plumage it is a common forager on suburban lawns in Hawaii.

After trudging some distance across the tundra in Denali National Park, I sat down on a ridge to have lunch. A few minutes later an American Golden-Plover ran rapidly by me without uttering a sound. It repeated this maneuver a few more times, then settled on its eggs not more than 10 feet away. I had no idea its nest was so close. I took this photo, packed up, and left without flushing the plover.

A loud whistle, sounding like *queed-lee*, which echoes across the tundra ridges, usually signals the golden-plover's presence. Sometimes a small number fly about and call as you near their nesting areas. Or sometimes you see one on a distant ridge, like a sentinel, silhouetted against the sky and silently watching.

⌒ OYSTERCATCHERS ⌒

These large shorebirds have a long, sturdy red bill that is flattened laterally. The bill tip is shaped like a chisel.

Black Oystercatcher
Length: 17 in.

The Black Oystercatcher is a resident bird along the Pacific Coast from the Aleutians to Baja California, but nowhere is it abundant. The breeding population for Alaska is roughly estimated at 5,000 to 6,000 birds and accounts for about 60 percent of the world's population.

This crow-sized, all-black-bodied shorebird has a long red bill and pinkish legs and feet. It is sometimes noisy, calling with a loud, whistled *wheee-whee-whee-whee*.

The Black Oystercatcher uses its specialized flattened bill to obtain food in interesting ways. With the chisel-like tip, it can pry chitons, limpets, and barnacles from rocks. This tip also allows the birds to insert the bill into partly open and feeding bivalves, such as mussels and clams, while they are underwater. The oystercatcher quickly severs the adductor, the strong muscle holding the bivalve's two shells together, before the shells can be closed. If the oystercatcher finds a closed bivalve, it may hammer a hole in the shell with rapid, powerful blows of its bill, then sever the muscle by inserting its bill through the hole. Young oystercatchers learn these specialized feeding techniques by watching their parents, and they may stay with their parents for up to a year.

～ SANDPIPERS ～

Sandpipers are mostly ground-dwelling wading birds that frequent the shorelines of our ocean, lakes, ponds, and rivers. During spring and fall migrations, most are gregarious and fly about in large flocks often composed of several species. When flushed, they fly in remarkably close formation, all seeming to turn, rise, and alight together as one.

Most of our sandpipers do not build much of a nest. A shallow, unlined depression on the ground in moss, grass, or gravel is typical. The Solitary Sandpiper has the unusual habit of laying its eggs in the abandoned tree-nests of other birds, such as those of the American Robin or Rusty Blackbird.

Most sandpipers practice a monogamous mating system, with the male and female establishing a pair bond and sharing the incubation of the eggs and the feeding and protection of their young. But Pectoral Sandpipers lack a pair bond. The Pectoral Sandpiper males establish territories and court females by inflating air sacs on either side of the upper breast and throat, enabling them to give a booming or hooting mating call. After mating, sometimes with several males, the female incubates the eggs and cares for the young by herself.

Spotted Sandpipers and Red-necked and Red Phalaropes practice a type of polyandrous mating system rare for birds. After mating and laying eggs, the female leaves the male to incubate the eggs and rear the young. She may repeat this process with other males. One species, the Sanderling, lays one clutch of eggs to incubate herself and another for the male.

Western Sandpiper

Greater Yellowlegs
Length: 14 in.

Both the Greater and Lesser Yellowlegs, with their long legs, are some of the easiest sandpipers to observe. During nesting they will even come to you. Standing on top of a tree or snag, they give an unending shrill alarm call until you depart from their muskeg or marsh. Their call notes help to distinguish the two species of yellowlegs. The Greater Yellowlegs gives a 3- or 4-note whistle, *whew-whew-whew*, and the Lesser Yellowlegs a 1- or 2-note call, *tew-tew*.

The Greater Yellowlegs is the only sandpiper to feed extensively on fish. They can be seen in shallow tidal sloughs as they rush rapidly about in short bursts after small staghorn sculpins, which they gulp down whole. They also fish by wading in the water while swinging their bills from side to side.

The Lesser Yellowlegs (about 3 inches shorter) will also eat small fish, but it feeds more on insects and other invertebrates. In the freshwater marshes and muskeg ponds, they go after dragonfly larvae, water boatmen, diving beetles, and various flies. The Lesser Yellowlegs snatches food with its bill and does not swing its bill from side to side.

Wandering Tattler
Length: 11 in.

As a breeding bird, the Wandering Tattler is more abundant in Alaska than elsewhere. Some have been reported nesting in the Yukon, northwestern British Columbia, and in northeastern Siberia, but the tattler is considered largely an Alaskan bird. It breeds along the rock-strewn mountain streams above timberline and lays eggs within a hollow among the streamside gravel and rocks. Some build a nest of roots, twigs, and leaves.

Tattlers often feed by wading in these mountain streams and probing under rocks for aquatic insects. They also search for food within the small seeps and marshy areas associated with these streams. They seem rather tame while breeding, but are very difficult to see. With their sometimes quiet nature and gray plumage, which blends in well with the boulders of their habitat, they easily go unnoticed.

During migration and in winter, when these birds may congregate, they can be quite noisy, giving a loud 3-note whistle. At this time they live up to their name and wander widely, to some of the remotest islands in the Pacific, Australia, New Zealand, and Japan, and from central California south to Ecuador. They rarely associate closely with other sandpipers and are often seen alone or in pairs and small groups when they frequent the more rocky saltwater beaches.

Surfbird
On nest. Length: 10 in.

These stocky shorebirds spend most of the year along the rocky shores of the Pacific Coast. They forage among the rocks, often with the surf crashing around them. For nesting, however, Surfbirds choose the rocky alpine areas in Alaska. They blend in well with this habitat and, except when courting, are usually silent. Few nests have ever been found.

Finding a Surfbird nest was a birding highlight for me. It was quite by accident. While hiking along a mountain ridge above Wonder Lake, adjacent at that time (June 1978) to Denali National Park, I nearly stepped on a Surfbird incubating its eggs. Had the bird not flushed, my next step would have surely crushed it. Fifty-two years earlier, in 1926, the first recorded Surfbird nest was discovered in much the same way by George W. Wright, who also found it on a bare alpine ridge in Denali National Park. Since then only a few humans have ever laid eyes on a Surfbird nest and to my knowledge no one, at that time, had ever photographed a surfbird on its nest.

Marking the nest with a rock cairn, I returned with a portable blind and set it up about 100 feet away from the nesting bird. I intended to move it closer each day, so the bird would get used to it. After several days, the blind was finally close enough for me to photograph the Surfbird. It was a warm, sunny day, so I decided to see how close I could get. I stopped 3 feet away, and it never flushed. No wonder so few nests have been found!

Red-necked Phalarope
Male. Length: 7 in.

The Red-necked Phalarope is a small sandpiper that swims with ease. Male and female phalaropes practice a reversal of the normal parent roles. The female is larger and more colorful than the male. The breeding female, gray above, with rufous coloring on the neck and a white throat, displays and calls to attract the male. After laying her eggs, she repeats her displays and calling and leads the male to the nest. He then incubates the eggs and cares for the young, and the female leaves.

The male phalarope, browner than the female and with a white eye-line, even develops brood patches on his abdomen, where he loses feathers and the skin thickens and becomes engorged with blood to help warm the eggs. The female phalarope does not develop brood patches.

Phalaropes are the only members of the sandpiper family that spend the winter on the open ocean. Red-necked Phalaropes from Alaska winter in the South Pacific and possibly off the coast of Peru and in the East Indies.

— JAEGERS, GULLS, TERNS —

Jaegers live up to their German name, which means "hunter." Called a sea falcon by some, these birds are efficient predators of songbirds, shorebirds, lemmings, and the eggs and young of other birds. They also chase other seabirds and cause them to disgorge their food, which the jaeger, an agile flier, catches in midair. The Parasitic Jaeger is known to join migrating Arctic Terns to pirate food from them during their long journeys. Jaegers also scavenge, following ships to feed on garbage thrown overboard and the waste from fish-processing ships.

Gulls will eat almost anything. They scavenge the beaches, and some species frequent garbage dumps in large numbers. Gulls can act as predators, especially within and near their nesting colonies, where they prey on other gulls' eggs and young as well as the eggs and young of other bird species that nest near their colonies.

Some gulls are quite innovative in obtaining food. Glaucous-winged Gulls carry mussels, clams, and sea urchins aloft, dropping them on the rocks below to crack their shells. I have seen them wading in streams among spawning salmon, where they induce the female to extrude her eggs by punching her belly with their beaks, then quickly move to the salmon's vent to catch and eat them.

Terns are more selective in their diet and feed mostly on fish. They typically look for fish by hovering over the water, bills pointed downward. Terns usually plunge headfirst after their prey or pick the smaller ones from the surface. They also eat squid, shrimp, crabs, and insects.

Black-legged Kittiwake, immature

Long-tailed Jaeger
Length: 21 in.

This bird is the smallest of the 3 species of jaegers that occur in Alaska. The adult has long, streaming tail feathers. The abundance of breeding Long-tailed Jaegers and their nesting success are closely tied to the abundance of their prey. In years of high populations of voles and lemmings, more of these birds breed; in such years they usually lay 2 eggs instead of 1, and more young survive.

Although they seem to prefer small mammals, Long-tailed Jaegers will prey on nearby nesting songbirds, especially Lapland Longspurs, as well as on the young of plovers and sandpipers. They feed insects to their young for a short time immediately after hatching. As the chicks grow, the adults feed them small mammals. But young jaegers cannot handle an entire mammal the size of a lemming, and a single adult cannot tear one apart. So, the two parents butcher the lemming cooperatively, tearing it apart using a tug-of-war technique.

During migration and in winter, Long-tailed Jaegers spend most of their time well offshore and thus are seldom seen, except on their northern breeding grounds, by land-based bird-watchers. They winter mostly at sea off the coast of South America from Ecuador to Chile.

Mew Gull
On nest. Length: 17 in.

The Mew Gull is the smallest of the commonly seen white-headed gulls, but among gulls occurring in Alaska it would be considered medium-sized. The name comes from a mewing call they give mainly on their breeding grounds. Mew Gulls are the most widely distributed gull in Alaska, and they are common everywhere except the northern region, where they are considered rare. Mew Gulls and Glaucous-winged Gulls are the ones we most often see here in winter.

Like the Glaucous-winged Gull, the Mew Gull has evolved some interesting methods of obtaining food. They fly aloft with sea urchins and drop them on the rocks below to break their shells. On salmon streams I have seen them rapidly moving their feet up and down to create a sort of upwelling current that brings salmon eggs to the surface, where they are more easily eaten. They also do this in tidal pools to raise invertebrates to the surface from the mud and vegetation.

Some Mew Gulls are solitary nesters, and some breed in small colonies. They typically nest on islands or on level ground near streams, lakes, or ponds, but may also nest in trees, on stumps, and within cavities in the sand.

Arctic Tern
With young. Length: 15 in

Arctic Terns have long, pointed wings, a forked tail, black cap, and a bright red bill and feet. They nest in colonies, usually in areas with little or no vegetation, near sources of fish. One only need approach a colony of nesting terns to observe how vigorously they defend their nesting grounds. Usually they start diving at you and giving their piercing *tearrr* call long before you are very near. To deter them, and to protect yourself, raise a stick above your head for them to attack. I have only been hit once by an Arctic Tern, in the forehead. It hurt, drew blood, and made me more cautious.

I have visited the same Arctic Tern colony over the last 30 years. I have sometimes photographed from a blind or just observed. I have seen newly hatched chicks emerge from beneath one parent to accept fish from the other parent before it lands. These young terns apparently could recognize their own parents' voices among the many terns constantly circling and calling from above the colony. Studies of certain colonial nesting seabirds have shown that while still in the egg, the chicks learn to distinguish the parents' voices from others in the same colony.

— ALCIDS —

About 33 million alcids are thought to breed in Alaska every year. These include the murres, guillemots, murrelets, auklets, and puffins. Alcids are adapted to life on and beneath oceanic waters, coming to land only for nesting. These birds use their wings to "fly" underwater, and use their webbed feet only for steering or for swimming on the surface. Their legs are set far back on their bodies, and they have a lurching, penguinlike gait on land.

Most of the species nest in colonies, which may consist of tens of thousands of birds, on a small island or coastal cliff. Some species nest in close proximity, each adapted to a special niche that minimizes competition. Pigeon Guillemots may nest among boulders near the water. A little higher up, Parakeet, Crested, and Least Auklets may nest deep within the rubble of talus slopes. Common and Thick-billed Murres may choose the cliff ledges jutting out along the more vertical part of the cliff. Near the top, where the soil begins, Tufted Puffins usually dig their nesting burrows. Other seabirds such as kittiwakes, storm-petrels, and gulls may be interspersed, each occupying its own special place. Variations occur, but one of the wondrous sights in the bird world is to see so many different species in such huge numbers, in one relatively small area.

While most birds suffer from destruction of their nesting habitat by humans, Alaska's alcids are relatively well protected. The Alaska Maritime National Wildlife Refuge includes an enormous number of offshore islands, islets, rocks, reefs, and spires, including many of the Aleutian Islands. All are used by nesting alcids. They face different threats to their existence, however, through oil spills, gill nets, and competition with humans for food. Introduced predators such as rats and foxes are a problem on some islands.

The human demand for fish most often eaten by alcids has been increasing. For example, Common Murres on the Seward Peninsula have decreased in proportion to the increased pressure by commercial fisheries on walleye pollock (now used to make imitation crab) in the southeastern Bering Sea.

Marbled Murrelet

Length: 9 ½ in.

At the more northern limit of their range in Alaska, Marbled Murrelets have been found nesting on the ground in rocky, unvegetated areas. But throughout most of this bird's range, in Alaska as well as elsewhere, they are thought to nest in the thick, luxuriant moss found on the branches of old-growth coniferous trees. The birds' dependence on old-growth trees may relate to this moss, on which females lay a single egg. According to one report, this moss does not appear on large branches of conifers of the Pacific Northwest until the forest is 150 or more years old. The birds' access to nesting sites may require the open-crown structure found in these old-growth trees but not in second-growth timber. Marbled Murrelets, like all alcids, have short, narrow wings better designed for underwater pursuit of fish than for aerial maneuvering and landing in tight places.

Like the Spotted Owl, murrelets are considered to be at risk from the logging of these ancient coniferous forests. Their numbers have been declining in Washington, Oregon, and California, where the bird has been listed as a threatened species under provisions of the Endangered Species Act.

Horned Puffin

Length: 14 ½ in.

Their massive bills, with bright oranges, yellows, and reds, make puffins one of the most bizarre-looking and colorful birds in Alaska. Tufted Puffins are named for their pale-yellow ear tufts. Horned Puffins derive their name from the stiff, black, fleshy projections above each eye.

The beaks of most birds are covered with a single horny sheath that is renewed as it is worn down. In puffins, however, this sheath thickens into several plates, which are shed during the molt after the breeding season. These large, vividly colored beaks are thought to function only as ornaments for courtship. After breeding, puffins' bills are smaller and less colorful. This reduction in beak size does not hinder their ability to catch and hold fish, as the serrations on the inside of the upper mandible and the spines on the tongue remain year-round.

The North American breeding puffin populations are estimated at about 4 million for the Tufted and 1.5 million for the Horned Puffin. Most breed in Alaska. Tufted Puffins prefer to excavate their own burrows, which may be as long as 6 feet, in the soil. Horned Puffins prefer to nest in crevices in the rocks. Where they occur together, these different nest site preferences help reduce competition.

These short-legged birds have pointed wings and a small, rounded head that they bob when walking. Only the Rock Dove is common in Alaska. Band-tailed Pigeons and Mourning Doves occur here but are considered rare.

Rock Dove
Length: 13 in.

The Rock Dove lives only in cities in Alaska and was originally introduced by humans. Rock Doves are the legendary homing pigeons. To find their homes, they can use many guidance systems including the sun's position and the earth's magnetic field.

Considered a pest by some, Rock Doves bring pleasure and amusement to others. Some people put food out especially for them; others sit in parks and sidewalk cafes and throw them scraps. The male Rock Dove always seems to be courting, with his neck inflated and tail spread, bowing and cooing while pursuing and circling a female on the ground.

To feed their young, Rock Doves, like all pigeons, regurgitate a creamy substance called pigeon's milk, which comes from the shedding of cells within the lining of the crop. This milk is very nutritious, containing more protein and fat than cow or human milk, and is rich in calcium and vitamins as well.

⸺ TYPICAL OWLS ⸺

If a mouse or vole squeaks, rustles in the leaves or dry grass, or chews its food, these sounds alone may be sufficient for an owl to find it. Owls have special adaptations enabling them to hear and locate their prey without actually seeing it. They include facial discs of stiff feathers, and fleshy erectile ear flaps for concentrating sounds and funneling them into the ears, a right ear opening shaped differently from the left for help in locating sounds, and specialized, sound-sensitive cells within the midbrain.

The owl's prey cannot hear its approach. Some owls have wing feathers with a serrated leading edge, unlike the smooth edge found in other birds' feathers. This characteristic helps muffle their wing noise in flight. Also, surfaces of flight feathers are very soft and downy. Silent flight may also help the owls hear their prey.

Of owls found in North America, Alaska has the heaviest (Snowy Owl), the most powerful (Great Horned and Snowy Owl), and the largest owl in height and wingspan (Great Gray Owl). We hear owls more often than we see them. Some that nest in Alaska begin calling and courting as early as winter. The series of deeply resonant *hoo* notes given in sets of 5 or 8 by the Great Horned Owl, the deep *hoooo* note given at irregular intervals by the Great Gray Owl, and the soft, bell-like call of the Boreal Owl are familiar late winter to early spring sounds to many Alaskans living in rural areas.

Great-horned Owl

The owl's diet is one of the easiest to establish. They usually swallow their prey whole and regurgitate the undigested fur, feathers, bones, bills, and teeth in well-formed, amazingly odorless pellets, which can be examined to identify the owl's prey.

Snowy Owl
Juvenile. Length: 22–25 in.

In Alaska, these large white owls nest on the open coastal tundra, from the western Aleutians to the arctic and subarctic tundra of northern Alaska. Their numbers fluctuate considerably, common in one area of Alaska one year and rare the next.

The Snowy Owl's abundance is closely tied to the population of lemmings, their major prey. They will overwinter in the Arctic if lemmings are sufficiently numerous. Otherwise they wander widely to the south in search of food. They also take voles, ground squirrels, ducks, young geese, gulls, and ptarmigan. In winter they have been observed preying on eiders and Oldsquaws a considerable distance from shore in open areas among the sea ice.

The white plumage of these owls provides them with maximum insulation against the arctic cold. As is true of the white feathers of ptarmigan, their feathers contain no pigment, allowing more space for air, the best insulator. Snowy Owls also have completely feathered feet with extra-thick pads on the soles for insulation.

Snowy Owls nest on the slightly elevated hummocks found scattered throughout the tundra. Only the female incubates the eggs, and the male brings her food and defends the nest from predators. Both male and female continue to feed the young after they have all left the nest.

Short-eared Owl
Length: 15 in.

This owl's buffy-brownish color and mothlike, flapping flight with very deep wing strokes help identify it. The somewhat similar-looking Northern Harrier inhabits the same kinds of open areas the Short-eared Owl prefers, but it has a conspicuous white rump patch that the Short-eared Owl lacks.

This is the most common and most easily observed owl in Alaska. The Short-eared Owl often hunts during daylight, and you may even see it in the midafternoon sunshine in open areas such as salt marshes and tundra.

The Short-eared Owl spends most of its time on the ground or hunting in the air. Only occasionally do we see them perched on fence posts or in trees. They roost on the ground and usually conceal their nests at ground level in sedges or tall grass.

In spring the male conducts rather elaborate courtship displays. He flies up and up in slow, easy curves while giving a call resembling rapid basslike toots. Sometimes starting from a considerable height, he then flies down in short, slanting dives that end in an upward swoop. During each dive he rapidly claps his wings together under his body, making sounds like a flag fluttering in a stiff wind.

Swifts resemble swallows, but their wings are narrow, slightly decurved, and held very stiffly. In flight they appear to beat the wings alternately, but this is an illusion.

Vaux's Swift
Length: 4 in.

Smaller than any of Alaska's swallows, with no apparent tail and pale brown underparts, this bird is found on a regular basis only in southeastern Alaska. These birds spend more time in the air than most other birds. While flying they feed, drink water, bathe, gather their nest materials, and mate. They have strong claws for clinging to vertical surfaces and probably never intentionally land on the ground.

The Vaux's Swift makes its small saucer-shaped nest of twigs and spruce needles and glues it with saliva to the inside wall of a hollow tree. Outside Alaska, this species is beginning to utilize chimneys for nesting sites in the more populated areas, probably as a result of losing so much natural habitat. We most often see them flying quite high, sometimes over the treetops and sometimes over water in search of insects.

— HUMMINGBIRDS —

These tiny birds are known for their ability to hover and fly backward while rapidly beating their wings. Their long, slender bills and extensile tongues are especially adapted for sipping nectar from flowers.

Rufous Hummingbird
Male. Length: 3 ½ in.

Rufous Hummingbirds leave their winter home in Mexico in late February to early March and begin arriving in Alaska by mid-April. The brightly colored males arrive first and begin their courtship displays as soon as the females arrive. After courtship and mating, the male leaves the nesting and rearing of young to the female. By late June most males have left Alaska; most females and young leave in August.

Many flowers depend on hummingbirds for pollination. Such flowers typically produce little or no scent (which would attract insects). They have projecting stamens and pistils that touch the crown of the visiting hummingbird, depositing pollen on its head. These flowers also lack the landing platforms needed by bees. In addition, they are usually red (a color bees cannot perceive) and hold large quantities of nectar at the base of a long tube. Flowers thus structured specifically to attract birds as pollinating agents are termed "ornithophilous." In Alaska, the western columbine and Indian paintbrush have floral characteristics associated with hummingbird pollination. It is interesting that the distribution of columbine, common throughout southeastern and southcoastal Alaska, here closely coincides with that of the Rufous Hummingbird.

~ KINGFISHERS ~

Only one species, the Belted Kingfisher, occurs in Alaska. These birds catch fish by diving into the water head first. When fish are scarce they may feed on insects, small rodents, and even berries.

Belted Kingfisher
Length: 13 in

We usually first become aware of the Belted Kingfisher by its loud, rattling call. Both sexes have a blue-gray band across the breast. Females have an additional rufous-colored band and flanks, making them one of the few North American female birds that are more colorful than the male.

These kingfishers nest by digging a burrow into the cut banks of rivers, lakes, gravel pits, and even banks along highways and railroads, often near but sometimes distant from water. The burrows are usually 3 to 7 feet long and about 3 to 4 inches in diameter. At the end of the burrow, they build a nest chamber about 6 by 10 inches.

After catching a fish, these birds typically return to a perch and stun or kill the prey by beating it against the limb. Afterwards they may toss the fish into the air and swallow it head-first. When their young leave the nest, the parents must teach them how to fish. They usually accomplish this task by refusing to feed them, and instead drop stunned fish into the water until the young fly down to retrieve them. When the young can catch live fish on their own, which they learn to do in about 10 days, the parents drive them away from their territory.

⌐ WOODPECKERS ⌐

Woodpeckers are highly specialized for climbing the trunks and branches of trees and for digging out wood-boring insects. They have a number of adaptations for this specialized feeding. Short legs, strong toes, and sharp, curved claws enable them to climb vertical surfaces. A central pair of tail feathers is especially stiff, and the bird uses it to brace its body against the tree trunk. These feathers are so important in the bird's overall actions that they are not molted until new ones have grown in. The muscles of their skull, bill, and neck are stronger than those of most other birds. Their extra-long tongue with a barbed tip and their sticky saliva assist in the extraction of insects from holes. Woodpeckers are also thought to be capable of hearing insects moving or gnawing within or beneath the bark of trees.

Black-backed Woodpecker, barbed tongue

Wood-boring insects are active and available all year-round, so most of our woodpeckers overwinter in Alaska. The 2 species that leave the state, sapsuckers and flickers, have different feeding habits, which may explain their absence in winter.

Besides vocalizing, woodpeckers establish territories by loud drumming, usually on resonant hollow trees. In contrast, a feeding woodpecker may rather quietly chip away pieces of bark while looking for insects. I once nailed a wooden model of a Black-backed Woodpecker on a tree near Fairbanks and played a recording of one drumming. The male in whose territory I did this responded by viciously pecking the model on the head until he knocked it to the ground.

Red-breasted Sapsucker

At sap tree. Length: 9 in.

The male and female of all other woodpecker species in Alaska differ in appearance, but male and female sapsuckers look alike. The adults are distinguished by a red hood that covers the head, neck, and breast, and a long white stripe that goes down the folded wing. Their tongue is much shorter than those of other woodpeckers, and it has a brush-like tip for lapping up sap. The Red-breasted Sapsucker is found on a regular basis only in southeastern Alaska.

Sapsuckers are responsible for the rows of holes that we frequently see on the trunks of alder, cottonwood, and willow trees. They drill these holes through the bark to feed on the soft cambium layer just under it and on the sap that later oozes into and from these holes. They seem to be quite fond of this sugary sap and will guard the sap trees they have claimed and attempt to drive other birds away from them. Hummingbirds, warblers, and kinglets are attracted to the oozing sap as well as red and flying squirrels. Insects get stuck in the sap, providing the sapsucker with additional nutrition. The young are fed sap as well as insects and fruit. They learn from their parents the art of obtaining sap, while they are still clinging to the tree as fledglings.

In addition to the more traditional woodpecker methods of obtaining food, the Red-breasted Sapsucker snatches insects from the air in flycatcher fashion.

Flycatchers typically perch in an upright position on bare branches and make frequent short flights after flying insects, usually returning to the same perch. They have broad, flat bills especially adapted for catching insects.

Olive-sided Flycatcher
Length: 7 ½ in.

If an Olive-sided Flycatcher is courting or nesting nearby, you will know it. A loud, emphatic, whistled *whip-three-beers* echoes for some distance in the coniferous forests where they nest. No other bird sounds like it. These flycatchers are best distinguished by a narrow white stripe separating darker vestlike areas on the chest.

Other types of flycatchers are difficult to identify. Especially difficult are flycatchers belonging to the genus *Empidonax*. They look so similar that most bird-watchers can identify them only by their calls. Their generic name comes from the Greek words *empidos*, a gnat or mosquito, and *anax*, a king, lord, or master. These "mosquito kings" are very skilled at catching mosquitoes, and I like to have them around. The species you are most apt to see in Alaska are Alder, Hammond's, and Pacific-slope Flycatchers.

Other flycatchers commonly found here are the Western Wood-Pewee, which looks similar to *Empidonax* but lacks their white eye-ring, and the Say's Phoebe, with its distinctive cinnamon-colored belly and black tail.

Larks are sparrow-sized ground birds that rarely perch in the trees or bushes. They are famous in the field and in poetry for their complex and melodious songs.

Horned Lark
Length: 7 ½ in.

Adult Horned Larks have a distinctive pattern of black about their head and neck. The two small black "horns" (actually tufts of feathers) that give the bird its name are not always visible.

Horned Larks nest on the dry tundra of Alaska's mountains and foothills, although in migration we often see them foraging among the drier areas of tidal flats or along mountain ridges, sometimes with Lapland Longspurs. Female larks incubate the eggs and brood the young, while the male defends their territory. The young leave the nest with only partially developed flight feathers and no tail. They disperse in all directions, and the parents locate them for feeding by their calling. This early abandonment of the nest is common with most small, ground-dwelling birds, especially those that nest in the Arctic and open areas, where a noisy bunch of young in one spot would attract predators.

Male Horned Larks have a very distinctive courtship flight. First they fly up from the ground to a considerable height, perhaps 800 feet. Then they fly in a circle giving a series of high-pitched, tinkling notes. When finished singing, they fold their wings and plummet to earth, pulling out of this dive only just in time to avoid impact.

— SWALLOWS —

Swallows are excellent flyers that capture insects on the wing. They have long, pointed wings, a flattish head, a small, flat bill, and a wide mouth, and most have notched or forked tails. They commonly perch on wires.

Cliff Swallow
At nest. Length: 5 ½ in.

Cliff Swallows build their gourd-shaped nests of mud, sometimes in huge colonies, under the eaves of buildings and on bridge supports. These nesting colonies are a common sight along the Alaska Highway and along roads within Alaska, especially in the Interior. They still use nat-ural cliffs as nesting sites, and a number of these can be found in Alaska, especially along rivers.

The Cliff Swallow is the most easily recognized swallow in Alaska. It has a white forehead, dark chestnut-colored throat, and a conspicuous buffy rump patch.

During egg-laying, these swallows engage in a behavior known as brood parasitism, in which some females lay eggs in the nests of other Cliff Swallows. The parasitic egg-laying females enter a nest while the owners are away and quickly, in less than a minute, lay an egg of their own. They have also been observed to carry an egg in their beak to the nest of another swallow (the only bird known to do this).

— JAYS, MAGPIES, CROWS —

This family probably contains the smartest birds in the world in terms of what appears to be deductive thinking. Their intelligence is evident in their ability to learn, and in their adaptability, use of language, social interactions, play, use of tools, and survival techniques. Ravens have thrown stones at humans climbing toward their nest. Crows have been observed using a stick to probe for nuts in a crevice. A Carrion Crow of northern Europe learned to pull up an ice-fisherman's line to obtain a meal of fish.

While many birds sing, these birds seem to talk. Thirty different vocalizations have been described for the ravens in Alaska. The catlike, mewing calls of Northwestern Crows or the deep, bell-like notes of the Common Raven always get our attention. They can also mimic the sounds of other birds. The Steller's Jay's imitation of a Red-tailed Hawk scatters birds at a feeder. I once heard one give a perfect imitation of a calling Bald Eagle. A male Steller's Jay courts the female with an amazingly musical whisper-song that seems to include parts of songs from many other species.

Jays, magpies, and crows are generalists, which helps them adapt to new situations, exploit whatever food is available, and thus survive. Their bills are thick enough to hammer and pry, yet slender enough to probe. Many species have a slight hook on the bill, allowing them to tear food more easily. They have specialized throat pouches and cavities for holding food. Since they like to cache food for later use, these pouches allow them to carry a lot more.

Caching food can be advantageous to birds that spend the winter and nest in Alaska. For example, the Gray Jay nests while winter still grips the land and food supplies are low. Their previously cached food will sustain them through the winter as well as provide food for their young. Gray Jays are also known to cache material for insulating their nests before winter sets in.

Gray Jay
("Camp Robber")

69

Northwestern Crow
With blue bay mussel. Length: 17 in.

Crows and ravens occur together along the more southern coastal areas of Alaska. They look alike, though crows are smaller, about 5 to 10 inches shorter than ravens. But this is not much help unless they are standing side by side. From the ground, a crow jumps directly into the air, whereas the heavier raven takes 2 or 3 hops to become airborne. The crow's common call is a *kaah,* whereas the raven's is a throatier *kraaak.*

Northwestern Crows are tied closely to Alaska's ocean beaches. While they venture into nearby thickets and explore our coastal villages and cities, we do not find them far inland. One of their favorite foods is the blue bay mussel, which they drop from aloft to break open on the rocks below. They also comb the beaches for anything edible, including periwinkles, amphipods, insects, dead fish and mammals, and refuse.

They nest in colonies, and the flock, often about 50 birds, stays together all year-round. Within the flock, individuals help each other find food, and they also cooperate to mob predators. When a pair is nesting, a nonbreeding yearling crow may serve as a helper. The helper acts as a sentinel, defends the territory, and sometimes feeds the young. In turn, the helper gets fed by the adults. In one study, nests with helpers averaged 2 fledglings each, while those without helpers averaged only 1.2 fledglings.

Common Raven
Length: 22–27 in.

You may see these birds anywhere and anytime in Alaska. Tidal flats, ocean beaches, old-growth forests, muskeg, tundra, rocky cliffs, mountaintops, glaciers, ice fields, light poles, sidewalks, boat harbors—all are raven habitat. No other bird is so widespread and occurs in so many different habitats as does the Common Raven.

Most Alaskans enjoy watching their behavior and listening to their varied and unusual calls. In courtship, which can begin in mid-January, we may see the male soaring, wheeling, and tumbling in the sky, or observe the male and female flying one above the other with their wingtips touching. At any time of the year, we may see pairs flying along when suddenly one flips on its back or does a barrel roll and lets out a call sounding like *kukuk*. I have watched them pass objects to each other in flight and had them "play" with me on a mountain ridge. We see pairs perched on a light pole preening each other, touching bills, and making wonderful gurgling, popping sounds.

Most birds and mammals that live year-round in the more northern areas of Alaska cope with the severe cold with more fur, more feathers, and more fat. The raven, however, keeps warm with a higher than normal resting metabolic rate. As the air temperature drops, the raven only slightly increases its metabolism. In other words, their internal heater is always on high.

These little 5-inch birds with their dark caps, dark bibs, and white cheeks readily come to feeders, especially those offering sunflower seeds. The Chestnut-backed Chickadee is the species most often seen in southcoastal and southeastern Alaska. Farther north, in the interior portions of the state, you most often see Black-capped and Boreal Chickadees. The Siberian Tit is an Old World species from Siberia that has become established in central and western Alaska. Considered rare, this bird is sought by bird-watchers who wish to increase their list of North American birds.

Black-capped Chickadee
Length: 5 in.

This chickadee usually excavates its own nest in partially rotten trees. In interior Alaska, where they are the most common, they prefer dense, deciduous forests containing the larger trees. They like birch trees for nesting because the bark remains firm while the inner wood becomes soft. The female incubates an average of 6 eggs for about 12 days. After hatching, the young remain in the nest for about 16 days. If disturbed while incubating, the female makes an explosive *hiss* sound, reminiscent of the sound a startled snake makes.

In late summer these birds gather into small flocks, establish a feeding territory of roughly 20 acres, and defend it against other flocks. At night the flock roosts together, often in a tree cavity, for warmth.

~ NUTHATCHES ~

These small, tree-climbing birds are the only ones that descend tree trunks head-down. They also move up trees and along the undersides of limbs. Long toes and sharp claws enable them to cling to and climb on vertical surfaces. The Brown-headed Nuthatch of the southeastern United States is the only North American bird to habitually use tools. It uses pieces of bark to pry off other bits of bark when looking for insects.

Red-breasted Nuthatch
Length: 4 ½ in.

This nuthatch is often detected first by its voice, a high, nasal *yank-yank-yank*. They will come to feeders that offer sunflower seeds. Other common names include devil-down head and topsy-turvy bird. The Red-breasted Nuthatch is particularly fond of conifer cone seeds. They often wedge their food in the tree bark and feed by breaking off pieces of it; they do not hold food with their feet, as chickadees do. They also search for insects on trees and will make short flights to catch flying insects.

Nuthatches are a rare to uncommon bird in southeastern and southcoastal Alaska, and they occur only occasionally elsewhere in the state. In some years, however, they can be quite common in the southern portions of Alaska, especially during fall and winter. This happens when the coniferous cone crops fail elsewhere, and the birds come here looking for food. These sudden, massive population shifts resulting in changes in distribution due to food shortages are termed "irruptions."

~ CREEPERS ~

Creepers are small, tree-climbing birds. Their long tail feathers, stiffened at the end, act like a prop when they are climbing. They have a long, slender curved bill for probing in bark crevices for food.

Brown Creeper
Length: 5 ½ in.

These little birds have a brown back speckled and streaked with white, so they are very difficult to see on tree bark. When alarmed they flatten themselves against a tree trunk, spread their wings, and remain motionless. Their presence can be determined by their faint, high-pitched call, *ts-ts*, which they often give while feeding.

Creepers typically search for insects by starting at the bottom of a tree and working upward in a spiral fashion; they then fly to the base of the next tree and repeat the pattern. They also look for food along the undersides of branches.

Creepers usually build a hammocklike nest out of moss, twigs, bark, and feathers behind strips of loose bark. At night they will roost on the side of a tree by clinging with their long claws.

They will sometimes come to a feeder supplied with chopped peanuts or suet. Peanut butter combined with cornmeal and melted suet dabbed onto the bark of a tree may also attract them.

CREEPERS

74

⮬ WRENS ⮬

Wrens are small, restless, brownish birds with sharp-pointed bills. They hold their tails straight up when not in flight.

Winter Wren
Length: 4 in.

Winter Wrens forage and spend much of their time in dense brush and among the roots of fallen trees. They are one of the few birds we encounter near the forest floor. Usually we become aware of their presence by their sharp 2-note alarm call. Careful searching may reveal a tiny brown bird nervously bobbing up and down and scolding from an exposed perch at about eye level or lower. In spring, early summer, and sometimes fall, their beautiful, bubbly song can fill the forest. Their song has been reported to contain up to 113 separate notes!

Although they like the heavily forested areas over most of their range, in the treeless Aleutian and Pribilof Islands they feed among the beach rocks and nest in the cliffs and talus slopes. Elsewhere they nest among the roots of fallen trees, and in old stumps, brush piles, and abandoned buildings. For unknown reasons, the male often builds up to 4 "dummy" nests. Perhaps it gives the female more choices and enhances the male's success in attracting them. Wrens have been observed leading predators (Steller's Jays) to these dummy nests.

— DIPPERS —

Dippers are the only true aquatic songbirds in the world. They are stocky, wrenlike birds with special adaptations for feeding underwater.

American Dipper
Length: 7 ½ in.

The American Dipper is a permanent resident over most of Alaska. They can be found along almost any clearwater stream, even in winter along the North Slope, where air temperatures commonly dip to 40 below zero! In these arctic portions of Alaska, they seek out the warmer, springfed areas of rivers.

In search of aquatic insects, dippers walk underwater against a strong current and swim from one place to another. They walk by grasping stones with their long toes and by keeping their heads down, so the pressure of the running water helps force them against the bed of the stream. Underwater photography has revealed that they also use their wings to propel themselves.

Like other songbirds, the American Dipper declares or stakes out its territory by singing, even during winter—a trait unusual for any songbird in Alaska. Both sexes sing year-round. Their melodious song is especially delightful to hear during the otherwise almost silent Alaskan winter. I have often heard them while cross-country skiing, and once I timed a dipper's midwinter song nonstop for 15 minutes.

— OLD WORLD WARBLERS, KINGLETS, OLD WORLD FLYCATCHERS, THRUSHES —

Ruby-crowned Kinglet

Worldwide, this family contains over 1,400 species, and most are found in the Old World. Alaska has been host to 29 of these species, many accidental or rare, including such birds as Middendorff's Grasshopper-Warbler, Siberian Flycatcher, Siberian Rubythroat, and Red-flanked Bluetail. The more common species range from the unfamiliar Arctic Warbler to the more familiar Ruby-crowned Kinglet and to the very familiar American Robin. Most members of this family are fine singers, especially the thrushes.

Old World Warblers are small, rather drab-looking birds with slender little bills. They lack conspicuous markings and are difficult to identify. The kinglets are tiny birds no longer than a hummingbird, but much rounder. Old World Flycatchers are fairly small birds with flattened bills designed to capture insects. Only 5 species have reached Alaska, and then only occasionally. The Thrushes are a diverse group and include the beautiful sky-blue (male) Mountain Bluebird, the seldom-seen Townsend's Solitaire, and the frequently heard Varied Thrush, all found in Alaska.

Some species have very distinctive voices that are easy to learn. The little Ruby-crowned Kinglet sings a very loud, warbling song that sounds like *tee-tee-tee, chur-chur-chur, teedadee-teedadee-teedadee*. The Swainson's Thrush is responsible for beautiful, flutelike phrases that start on one pitch and spiral up the scale. These birds often sing well into the evening. The Hermit Thrush sounds somewhat similar to the Swainson's, but its phrases spiral down the scale, a handy way to tell their voices apart.

Arctic Warbler
Length: 4 3/4 in.

When helping people look for birds in Denali National Park, I am often asked to find an Arctic Warbler. It's never easy, because they are such drab birds and they blend in well among the leaves of the willows that they frequent.

We usually locate them by listening for their song, a trill introduced by a note sounding like *zick*, or *zick-zick-zick*. I think of their trill as sounding raspier than the other warblers, with each note containing a *z* sound.

You will not see this bird in the Lower 48 states. Most Arctic Warblers that nest in Alaska migrate from their wintering grounds in the Philippines through eastern Asia and across the Bering Strait to Alaska, returning by the same route. They usually arrive later than most other birds, in early to mid-June.

Getting this photograph was a challenge. Along the Denali Highway, but not in the park, I attempted to attract an Arctic Warbler by playing a recording of one singing. Playing recorded birdsongs is not permitted within the park boundaries. Although they were abundant and singing everywhere, they would not come close enough for photography, even when I set up a blind near the recorder. In desperation I hung the recorder over the car's side mirror and played it. The birds' response was amazing! Some even tried to get into the car. Apparently cars, familiar forms to these birds, were not considered a threat, but a strange object like a blind was alarming enough to prevent their close approach.

Northern Wheatear

Female at nest site. Length: 6 in.

Breeding males have black wings, a black face patch, and gray back. Both male and female have a white rump patch and black-and-white tail pattern. They have a habit of frequently bobbing and fanning the tail. Their common name comes from the white rump, and is apparently a euphemism meaning "white arse" in the ancient Anglo-Saxon language.

For nesting, Northern Wheatears choose the tundra rock fields above timberline. They nest on the ground, usually in crevices under rocks. In Denali National Park, a pair nested under the same rock several years in a row. A few days after the young fledge the parents separate them, and each parent takes care of its own group for another 10 or 11 days.

Like the Arctic Warbler, the Northern Wheatear does not migrate into the Lower 48 states except as an occasional vagrant. The Alaskan wheatears migrate via Asia to spend the winter on the savannas of northern and eastern Africa. During migration they often occur along our beaches and within the nonforested areas of our coastal tundra, especially in areas bordering the Bering Sea.

Gray-cheeked Thrush
Length: 7 ½ in.

The Gray-cheeked Thrush, as the name implies, has grayish cheeks. Otherwise these birds are brownish to olive gray on their upper parts, and heavily spotted on a whitish breast. Their song is a nasal *wee-oh, chee, chee, wee-oh* that usually rises abruptly at the end. Their call note sounds like *wee-a*.

Gray-cheeked Thrushes are the most northerly breeding thrush in North America. In Alaska they are a common breeding bird in all northern areas where suitable habitat occurs. They especially prefer shrub thickets. They also migrate the farthest of any of our thrushes, wintering in South America, some as far south as Peru. They are considered a rapid migrant, making the 4,000-mile trip from Louisiana to northwestern Alaska in 1 month, or about 130 miles a day. Gray-cheeked Thrushes migrate from South America to Alaska via the Mississippi Flyway.

Gray-cheeked Thrushes, along with other birds such as Varied Thrushes and American Robins, are among the most important avian distributors of seeds in North America. By eating fruit and later passing the seeds intact, they aid in the regeneration and population structure of plants.

Varied Thrush

Female. Length: 9 ½ in.

The Varied Thrush somewhat resembles a robin in size, shape, and breast color; in fact, it has been nicknamed the Alaska robin. The male has a broad, black breast band while that of the female is gray. An orange line above the eye, black mask, and orange wing bars are its other distinguishing features.

Every spring I am asked, "What was that bird making . . . ?" and before the question is finished, I know that most people are inquiring about the weird voice of the Varied Thrush. They usually sing hidden from view in the dense conifers. They are also often quite numerous, and the forest seems alive with their sounds. If you whistle and hum at the same time on one pitch and then repeat it on a higher or lower pitch, you have a fair imitation of their voice. Their song has a penetrating quality that seems ventriloquial. Sometimes one will be singing quite close, but it sounds much farther away.

The Varied Thrush is most common as a nesting bird within the coniferous forests of Alaska. It also breeds in the alders bordering rivers and lakes, especially in the more northerly parts of the state. When they are feeding and during their migration, you may also see them on the tundra, muskegs, tidal flats, and beaches.

— WAGTAILS, PIPITS —

Wagtails and pipits are smallish, slim birds with long legs. They walk instead of hop, and wag their long tails back and forth, flipping them around (wagtails), or pumping them up and down (pipits). They all have white outer tail feathers.

If you want to add members of this family to the list of North American birds you have seen, then seeing them in Alaska is your best bet. Of the 9 species found here, only 1, the American Pipit, commonly migrates into the Lower 48 states. All others probably enter Alaska by crossing the Bering Sea or Bering Strait from Asia.

Yellow Wagtail
At nest. Length: 6 ½ in.

The Yellow Wagtail is a common breeding bird on the coastal tundra of western Alaska, the offshore islands, and the tundra of the northern foothills of the western Brooks Range. These birds winter in the East Indies and migrate to Alaska via eastern China.

Yellow Wagtails are easy to see and find in the tundra habitats where they nest. Their striking yellow underparts make them one of the most colorful of the tundra birds, and no other bird looks like them. Sometimes they will come to you and scold with a metallic-sounding alarm note. Their call is a loud, single note, *tzeep*, often given when they fly overhead.

Waxwings derive their name from a bright red waxy substance of unknown function that forms on the tips of their secondary wing feathers. It mostly forms in older birds, and ornithologists speculate it may help in choosing a mate. Pairs of older birds are more successful than younger birds at raising their young.

Bohemian Waxwing
Length: 8 in.

In Alaska we see Bohemian Waxwings most often in fall and winter, when they travel about in flocks looking for food. At this time they are nomadic—here today, gone tomorrow. They are particularly fond of the berries of mountain ash, both the cultivated and indigenous species. Several towns and cities in southern Alaska have the introduced European mountain ash, and flocks of Bohemian Waxwings will sweep through neighborhoods, gorging themselves and stripping the trees of their berries. We are usually first attracted to the buzzy calls that they give almost incessantly. One of their nicknames, the northern chatterer, is appropriate at this time. Their name "Bohemian" is thought to relate to their nomadic behavior.

Bohemian Waxwings are also fond of the seeds of paper birch in interior Alaska as well as insects. They capture insects flycatcher-fashion, by flying out from a perch, or like swallows, by circling high in the air to snatch them in flight.

As a breeding bird they are most common in central Alaska. Here they most often build their nests in spruce trees about 6 to 8 feet above the ground. I usually see them in the more open spruce woodlands, with scattered deciduous trees, near water—areas with abundant flying insects.

⚊ SHRIKES ⚊

Shrikes are predatory songbirds that kill voles, small birds, and large insects. They are the only songbird that consistently behaves like a hawk. The shrike's bill is built like a falcon's—hooked, with a sharp, toothlike projection near the tip. Its eyesight, like that of hawks, eagles, and falcons, is remarkably acute. They have been reported spotting a running mouse at 240 feet and a caged one at more than 600 feet. Shrikes are nicknamed butcher birds because of their habit of impaling their prey on thorns and barbed wire for later use.

Northern Shrike
Length: 10 in.

I have had two memorable experiences with Northern Shrikes—finding a nest, and hearing one sing. The nest was located about 10 feet above the ground in a willow. It seemed oversized for such a small bird and was lined with a dense layer of white ptarmigan feathers. The shrike's behavior was remarkably fierce. It hovered close to my head and gave a grating, shrieking call. On another occasion I heard a shrike, usually a silent bird, sing a beautiful nonstop song reminiscent of that of a canary, interspersed with the gurglings of a parakeet.

In Alaska, Northern Shrikes are reported to feed on adult songbirds before the snow melts, voles as the snow melts and the ground becomes exposed, bumblebees as the weather warms, and young voles and songbirds as they leave their nests.

Starlings are an Old World family of birds represented by 111 species worldwide. Two, the European Starling and Crested Myna, have been successfully introduced to North America.

European Starling
In winter plumage. Length: 5 in.

Early attempts to introduce starlings to the United States and Canada failed—except for one. The 60 birds released in New York's Central Park in 1890 and the 40 more released in 1891 took hold. From these 100 birds, the starling population in North America has grown to more than 200 million. European Starlings have done a considerable amount of harm in the Lower 48 states. They outcompete hole-nesters such as bluebirds and woodpeckers for homes, compete with native thrushes and waxwings for food, destroy grain crops, and are a pest to humans. Only time will reveal their effect in Alaska, where their numbers and distribution have been gradually expanding.

This bird's jaw muscles work backwards. They have more strength opening the bill than closing it, the opposite of most other birds. This enables them to more easily pry apart vegetation, thereby exposing prey such as insects. This unique adaptation is considered a major reason for their high survival rate in winter.

∼ VIREOS ∼

Vireos look somewhat like dull warblers, but have a heavier bill with a hooked upper mandible. They also move more slowly and deliberately when feeding than do the more active warblers. Twelve species occur in North America, but only 2 migrate to Alaska on a regular basis each year.

Warbling Vireo
Length: 5 in.

Warbling Vireos occur only in southeastern Alaska on a regular basis. They are most common along the mainland rivers and near the mouths of these rivers. We usually become aware of its presence by its warbling song, given persistently and with a distinctive up-and-down pattern. This song is often given by the male while on the nest.

The Red-eyed Vireo, the other species found in Alaska, also breeds only in southeastern Alaska, where it is considered rare. More than any other bird, they are victimized by parasitic cowbirds. Cowbirds lay their eggs only in the nests of other birds. The host birds then hatch and raise the much-larger cowbird young, which often causes the songbird nestlings to starve or be crowded out of the nest.

Parasitism of vireo nests by cowbirds is considered to contribute to the decline of vireos in the eastern United States. The cutting of forests on the East Coast has made the habitat more favorable for cowbirds, and they have increased considerably, to the detriment of vireos and other songbirds. Cowbirds are rare in Alaska, but their distribution is similar to that of our vireos.

⟶ WOOD WARBLERS, TANAGERS, SPARROWS, BUNTINGS, BLACKBIRDS ⟶

This diverse family is the largest family of birds in the world. A total of 150 species occurs in North America, and of these, 60 have been found in Alaska, including the Yellow Warbler, Western Tanager, Song Sparrow, Snow Bunting, and Red-winged Blackbird. Because many of these birds are so unlike one another in looks and habits, they are best discussed in groups.

Wood Warblers are small, active birds that feed mostly on insects. They have small, thin bills. In Alaska, most of them have varying degrees of yellow plumage. In spring and summer, males and females look different; the male has bright, flashy breeding plumage, but the female is duller. In fall, the plumage of both sexes becomes duller, and identification of sexes and even species becomes more difficult.

Of the tanagers, only the Western occurs regularly in Alaska. Despite the males' brilliant red, yellow, and black plumage, they are not often seen because of their secretive habits. Tanagers are larger than warblers and have thicker bills. They feed on insects and berries.

Sparrows are small, brownish, rather drab-looking birds with short conical bills designed for crushing seeds. They feed mostly on the ground.

Four species of buntings breed in Alaska. Two of them are the whitest sparrowlike birds in Alaska. The Snow Bunting is found throughout the entire state and forms large flocks both in migration and in winter. The McKay's Bunting is found only on the islands and coast of the Bering Sea. Buntings feed on the ground in open areas.

Red-winged and Rusty Blackbirds are the species in the blackbird group that you are most likely to see in Alaska. We are often first drawn to the loud ringing *ok-a-lee* call of the Red-winged and the creaking call, like a squeaky hinge, of the Rusty. The breeding males of these two species are mostly black. The male Red-winged Blackbird has distinctive scarlet and buff wing patches.

Yellow Warbler
Male feeding young. Length: 5 in.

Yellow Warblers are probably the most noticed warbler in Alaska. They breed in every region and are very common over much of the state. No other bird is so bright yellow in color. The adult male has bright yellow underparts, reddish streaks on the breast, and yellow patches on the tail. The adult female is yellow underneath, with faint reddish streaks.

The male Yellow Warbler has a fairly loud song for a warbler, a lively *sweet-sweet-sweet-setta-see-see-whew!* During courting and nesting they sing almost incessantly. For example, in 29 hours of observation, one male was reported to sing an average of more than once each minute. Since their nests are placed more or less near our eye level, the birds are more visible during their visits to it. They are not as shy as many other warblers.

The female Yellow Warbler takes about 4 days to build a beautiful nest, and does all the incubating of the eggs and brooding of the young. She may steal construction material from the nests of other Yellow Warblers. Where parasitism by cowbirds occurs, the female Yellow Warbler may build a second story over her eggs. Up to 6 stories have been found in Yellow Warbler nests, with cowbird eggs entombed in each layer. While all this is going on, the male sings and maintains the territory. After the young hatch, however, he helps feed them.

Northern Waterthrush
At nest. Length: 6 in.

We seldom see the Northern Waterthrush. Although widely distributed and common in many areas of Alaska, its drabness, habitat, and habits make it difficult to find. While other warblers are flitting through the trees looking for and chasing insects, the Northern Waterthrush is walking along the ground, usually in dense underbrush near water. It behaves more like a sandpiper, exploring the water's edge and even wading. Here these birds search for insects, crustaceans, molluscs, and small fish. While walking they bob their heads and frequently tilt their tails upward. This "teetering" habit helps to identify them.

Their nests are well hidden on the ground beneath logs, roots, stumps, and in mossy banks. Like most birds, they are very secretive when visiting the nest. I watched a nest for several hours while the parents were feeding their half-grown young. They would typically land on the ground some distance away and then run, mouselike, not directly toward the nest but in sort of zigzag fashion, often disappearing for a while and then suddenly appearing at the nest's entrance.

The Northern Waterthrush winters in Central and South America. They are one of the North American species considered at risk by tropical deforestation.

Golden-crowned Sparrow
Length: 6 ½ in.

The Golden-crowned is one of my favorite sparrows. They are large and of striking appearance, with a conspicuous golden crown bordered in black. They nest in fairly wild places and have an unusual and memorable song. When nesting, they do not seem nearly so abundant as many other sparrows, so finding one is more challenging.

I usually find them in the mountains among the taller willows or alders just above timberline. When singing, they perch on the tops of trees or on an exposed branch and, if not disturbed, are easy to spot. Their song has a haunting, weird quality to it. It normally consists of 3 high, whistled notes of minor tone running down the scale like "Three Blind Mice." Once heard it is easily remembered, and no other bird sounds similar. Early gold miners in Alaska nicknamed this bird Weary Willy. When carrying their heavy loads, these miners thought the Golden-crowned Sparrow's song sounded like "I'm so weary."

When migrating, they often occur with White-crowned Sparrows and will readily come to an offering of birdseed, especially if it is spread on the ground. Most of them winter in the western United States and southern British Columbia. They like to eat flowers and buds, and some gardeners consider them a pest.

Snow Bunting
Length: 6 ½ in.

Snow Buntings breed farther north than any other songbird, including the highest-latitude lands adjacent to the Arctic Ocean. For nesting they often choose rocky sites with little vegetation, including cliffs, rocky shores, tundra, and mountain ridges. At Prudhoe Bay they have adapted to nesting under buildings, pipeline supports, and other man-made structures, probably to escape predation from foxes. Elsewhere their nest sites are well concealed, usually occurring deep in the crevices of rocks and cliffs.

In winter they leave their most northerly breeding areas, many spending the winter in southern Canada and northern parts of the Lower 48 states. Those that choose to winter in Alaska gather in small flocks and forage for seeds along our beaches and salt marshes.

The closely related McKay's Bunting breeds and winters only in Alaska. They breed on islands in the Bering Sea and winter along the Bering Sea coast. Hybridization with Snow Buntings occurs on St. Lawrence Island, and some ornithologists consider the two to be the same species.

— FINCHES —

Finches resemble sparrows with their short, conical beaks designed for cracking open the seeds that are their main food. In contrast to sparrows, which feed mostly on the ground, most finches spend much of their time foraging in trees. Here they seek out the seeds produced in cones. Some species have specialized bills and methods for extracting these seeds. Others knock them out of the cones and eat them on the ground. The abundance of many finches is tied closely to the success or failure of the cone crop. The species that breed in Alaska also winter here.

Since the seeds of many plants found in Alaska remain on the plant well into the winter, finches often have an abundant above-snow food supply at this time. Most finches crush the seeds they eat, thus destroying them, so they do not help in plant dispersal like the fruit-eating thrushes, which swallow seeds whole and later pass them intact.

Red Crossbill

Pine Grosbeak
Length: 9 in.

The adult male has a very thick, stubby bill, rosy red plumage, and 2 white wing bars. The adult female's head and rump are tinged with yellow.

About the size of a robin, the Pine Grosbeak is the largest finch in Alaska. We see them most often in late fall and winter when, along with Bohemian Waxwings, they travel in flocks seeking the berries of the European mountain ash trees that grow within our cities and towns. Their loud, clear, 2- to 3-note whistle contrasts sharply with the buzzy calls of the waxwings.

Pine Grosbeaks can be very tame. In winter you can often walk to within a few feet of them while they are feeding. Even when nesting, they sometimes alight nearby. They will also come to an offering of sunflower seeds.

White-winged Crossbill
Length: 6 in.

Crossbills can be abundant in Alaska, but you may never see one. It helps to have a knowledge of their habitat, habits, and calls, and a good spotting scope. Flocks of small birds flitting about in the tops of coniferous trees may be crossbills. Here these birds seek the seeds produced within the cones. White-winged Crossbills like the seeds of spruce and may be found feeding wherever spruce forests occur in Alaska, crawling about the spruce cones like small parrots. A loud, harsh call sounding like *cheet, cheet*, given by many birds in the feeding flocks, helps us detect them.

To extract seeds, they insert their crossed mandibles between the bracts, open their bills to spread them apart, and extract the exposed seed with their tongues. This specialized bill allows these birds to utilize a resource that otherwise would not be available to them.

This specialization, however, makes crossbills dependent on the cone crops. Spruce trees are erratic in their production of cones—abundant one year, scant the next. Crossbills may wander widely in search of the best cone crops, and they stay around to nest and feed wherever they find a good cone crop. They may nest any time of the year, but most often January through April. The parents feed their young by regurgitating a milky pulp of spruce seeds.

Common Redpoll
Length: 5 in.

Common and Hoary Redpolls have a bright red cap, blackish chin, and a pinkish wash on their breast. The Common Redpoll has heavy streaking on the rump and flanks. The Hoary Redpoll has no streaking on the rump, few streaks on the flanks, and a very short bill. Much overlap occurs, and some ornithologists consider these two species to be the same.

Redpolls are common throughout the year over much of Alaska. In winter they are absent only from the northernmost part of the state.

Redpolls can tolerate more cold than most other songbirds. In Fairbanks you see flocks of these small birds feeding at temperatures as low as -40°F. A pocketlike modification of their esophagus, about midway down the neck, allows them to store seeds that they can later regurgitate, shell, and eat. They can gather food in exposed locations and later fly to a sheltered place to eat, and they can gather enough food toward the end of a short winter day to survive the long, cold night.

In winter, when the seeds from grasses, sedges, and weeds are covered with snow, redpolls depend on the seeds from the catkins of birches, willows, and alders that extend above the snow. To obtain these seeds they rather acrobatically knock them out of their catkins and later gather them up from the ground or snow below.

FINDING
ALASKA'S
BIRDS

Long-billed Dowitcher

To help Alaska residents and visitors find birds, I have listed some of the "hot spots" for bird-watching, organized by region (see map, pages 4-5). I have selected only those accessible by road, commercial airline, ferry, tour ship, and the more established tours conducted specifically for bird-watching. I have also included useful publications such as bird checklists, bird-finding guides, and general guidebooks.

A number of bird checklists cover selected areas of Alaska. Some suggest places to visit and tell you what habitats each species frequents. Most give the relative abundance of each species by season. Helpful information is also available in a few published bird-finding guides. I mention here all the guides and checklists of which I am aware—pamphlets of this sort, like the birds, are often here today and gone tomorrow, and new ones continually surface. In the case of local or privately issued lists, on-the-spot inquiries in each area you visit are the best way to determine their availability. Public libraries, visitor centers, and local bookstores and chambers of commerce are good places to begin looking.

Many areas of Alaska, including both state and federal refuges, have been set aside for the protection of its birds. In addition a number of national parks, monuments, preserves, forests, state parks, and game sanctuaries are good places to find birds. The excellent *Alaska's Parklands*, by N. L. Simmerman (The Mountaineers, Seattle, Wash., 1991) gives detailed information on these areas and includes useful addresses and telephone numbers. *A Guide to Wildlife Viewing in Alaska*, by S. E. Quinlan, N. Tankersley, and P. D. Arneson, of the Alaska Department of Fish and Game (1983), also gives addresses and telephone numbers of government agencies as well as a few private ones that can provide bird-finding information. (This publication also includes a number of the more remote birding areas not mentioned here.) For just getting around Alaska, the annual publications *The Milepost* and *The Alaska Wilderness Guide* (Vernon Publications, Bellevue, Wash.) are indispensable guides. For those traveling to Alaska via

Canada, I recommend J. C. Finlay, ed., A *Bird-Finding Guide to Canada* (Hurtig Publishers Ltd., Edmonton, Alberta, 1984).

Southeastern Alaska

This region is dominated by the Sitka spruce–western hemlock coastal forest. It consists of a narrow strip of mainland mountains, over 1,000 offshore islands, 21 wilderness areas encompassing about 43 percent of the region, and the nation's largest national forest, the Tongass. See *Birds of Southeast Alaska: A Checklist*, by P. Isleib et al. (Alaska Natural History Association, 1987).

Alaska Marine Highway: From the ferries and tour ships, you can see a variety of sea ducks, gulls, Marbled Murrelets, and Bald Eagles. When crossing areas on or near the open ocean, keep an eye out for seabirds such as shearwaters, storm-petrels, and fulmars.

Glacier Bay National Park and Preserve: From tour boats look for Tufted and Horned Puffins, Marbled and Kittlitz's Murrelets, Black-legged Kittiwakes, huge flocks of Red-necked Phalaropes (especially in August), various sea ducks, and Bald Eagles. See *Birds of Glacier Bay National Park and Preserve*, by Bruce Paige (Alaska Natural History Association and National Park Service, 1986).

Haines: Alaska Chilkat Bald Eagle Preserve is accessible by road 17 miles from Haines. Up to 3,500 Bald Eagles gather here, and the best months are October through December. See *Birds of Haines: A Checklist*, by Dan Bertsch (Haines, Alaska).

Juneau: In the Mendenhall Wetlands State Game Refuge, you can view Arctic Terns, Vancouver Canada Geese, waterfowl, and shorebirds from an easy 1.5-mile-long trail. (Access is at the end of Radcliff Avenue near the airport.) Juneau has a marvelous trail system. See *90 Short Walks Around Juneau*, by M. L. King (Taku Conservation and Juneau Audubon Societies, Juneau, 1987). See also *Juneau Trails* (Alaska Natural History Association, 1985), and *Birds of Juneau Alaska Checklist*, by G. van Vliet et al. (Juneau Audubon Society, 1993).

Petersburg: The Blind Slough Trumpeter Swan Management Area is 18 miles south of Petersburg on Mitkof

Highway. About 100 Trumpeter Swans winter here from late October to March. See *Checklist of the Birds of Mitkof Island*, by P. J. Walsh (1993).

Prince of Wales Island: This is a good place to find common birds of southeastern Alaska because of the variety of habitats that can be reached by nearly 200 miles of road. The Craig-Klawock area is recommended for sea ducks and shorebirds. See *Finding Birds on Prince of Wales Island*, by Thomas Kogut (USDA Forest Service, Craig Ranger District, 1984).

Sitka: Charter boats can take you to St. Lazaria Island, a part of the Alaska Maritime National Wildlife Refuge. Here you can see Tufted Puffins, the occasional Horned Puffin, Cassin's Auklet, Common and Thick-billed Murres, Pigeon Guillemots, and Rhinoceros Auklets.

Southcoastal Alaska

This region is dominated by the Sitka spruce-western hemlock coastal forest. It includes the largest contiguous wetland on the Pacific Coast of North America, the Copper River Delta. This area hosts millions of shorebirds during migration, offers unique opportunities to see nesting seabirds, contains one of the richest marine environments in the world (Prince William Sound), and offers opportunities to view birds associated with the open ocean.

Alaska Marine Highway: From Homer and Seward, the state ferry goes to Kodiak and Dutch Harbor, a trip offering great opportunities in Alaska to see birds associated with the open ocean— Short-tailed and Sooty Shearwaters, Fork-tailed Storm-Petrels, Northern Fulmar, the Black-footed Albatross, and many species of alcids (puffins, murres, auklets, and murrelets). The Laysan Albatross and Whiskered Auklet are species sometimes seen on the western part of this route.

Anchorage: At Potter Point State Game Refuge, ("Potter Marsh") about 10 miles from Anchorage on New Seward Highway, road pullouts offer looks at migrating and nesting waterfowl, Arctic Terns, gulls, and shorebirds. Other suggestions: Lake Hood/Lake Spenard, Earthquake Park, Campbell Airstrip, Chugach State Park, Westchester Lagoon, and the adjacent coastal trail. See *Birds of Anchorage, Alaska, A*

Checklist (Anchorage Audubon Society), and *Field Guide to Birding in Anchorage*, by R. L. Scher.

Cordova: At the Copper River Delta up to 20 million shorebirds gather in late April and May. There is road access to a few viewing areas—Hartney Bay and Alaganik Slough. Nesting Trumpeter Swans and the Dusky Canada Goose are sometimes seen from the road toward the airport. See *Birds of the Chugach National Forest*, by M. E. Isleib (USDA Forest Service, Alaska Regional Leaflet no. 69).

Homer: From here you can visit a wide variety of habitats and great birding areas. Charter boats and tours are available for visits to seabird nesting colonies. See *A Bird Finder's Guide to Homer and Kachemak Bay, Alaska*, by G. C. West (Birchside Studios, Homer, 1991), and *Birds of Kachemak Bay, Alaska*, by D. Erikson (Center for Alaskan Coastal Studies, Homer, 1983).

Kodiak: From the road system, it is possible to see Aleutian Terns and puffins. A variety of trails takes you to different habitats. See *Kodiak National Wildlife Refuge and Kodiak Island Archipelago Bird List*, by R. MacIntosh (Kodiak National Wildlife Refuge, 1986).

Seward: Charter boats can take you to the Chiswell Islands to view nesting seabirds. See *Birds of Seward, Alaska*, by J. Andrew et al. (Seward Chamber of Commerce, 1988).

Southwestern Alaska–Aleutian Chain

The southwestern region is almost treeless, being dominated by tundra, and under a strong marine influence that produces clouds, fog, and heavy precipitation. This region is a bird-lister's delight! Because of its nearness to Siberia, many species of Asiatic birds can be found here. Some have become regular breeders in the region.

Attu Island: Attu is located at the very end of the Aleutian chain. Over 200 species have been seen on Attu, including many Asiatics. Special birding tours are operated each year from about the middle of May to early June. See *Attu Island, Alaska, Checklist of Birds*, by L. G. Balch and T. G. Tobish (Attour, Inc. 1990), and "Birding Attu," by L. G. Balch, in *Birding* (February 1980).

Izembek National Wildlife Refuge: The largest expanse of eelgrass in the world attracts huge numbers of Brant,

Emperor Geese, Steller's Eiders, and numerous other water-fowl species. Access is via Cold Bay and a 10-mile road from town.

Pribilof Islands: Over 2 million seabirds nest on these islands, including Northern Fulmars, Red-legged Kittiwakes, Red-faced Cormorants, Horned Puffins, and Thick-billed Murres, Least, Crested, and Parakeet Auklets. Viewing blinds are available at the rookeries on St. Paul Island. Access to the blinds is available through packaged tours or by permit. St. George Island is the best for photographing birds. See "Birding the Pribilof Islands, Alaska," by S. T. Zimmerman and I. L. Jones, in *Birding* (23:5, 1991).

Central Alaska

Much of central Alaska is covered by a boreal forest consisting of white spruce mixed with Alaskan paper birch. Broad river valleys filled with lakes, bogs, and marshes provide some of the most important nesting habitat for the waterfowl of North America. The region also contains the highest mountains in North America. See *Bird Watching in Eastcentral Alaska*, by M. I. Springer (Falco Publication, Fairbanks, 1993).

Chena River Recreation Area: This area includes rivers, lakes, boreal forest, and alpine tundra. Trails lead into the alpine tundra. Here look for ptarmigan, Surfbirds, Lapland Longspurs, and Golden Eagles. Access is via the Chena Hot Springs Road out of Fairbanks, between mile 26 and mile 54.

Creamers Field Migratory Waterfowl Refuge: Ducks, geese, and Sandhill Cranes stop here during spring and fall migrations. A 2-mile nature trail winds through a variety of habitats. Access is off College Road about a mile north of downtown Fairbanks.

Denali Highway: This is one of my favorite areas to look for birds in central Alaska. The 135-mile road between Paxson and Cantwell covers terrain that includes tundra and birds similar to those found in Denali National Park. But here you have the freedom of using your own car, and if you like to photograph birds, there are no restrictions.

Denali National Park and Preserve: Many exciting birds can be seen alongside and within an easy walk of the park road. These include Harlequin Ducks, Oldsquaws, Willow and Rock Ptarmigan, American Golden-Plovers, Wandering Tattlers, Whimbrels, Long-tailed Jaegers, Arctic Warblers, and Northern Wheatears. See *Bird-Finding Guide to Denali National Park*, by K. Kertell and A. Seegert (1985), and also *Bird Checklist for Denali National Park*, by K. Kertell (1984). (Both are published by the Alaska Natural History Association and National Park Service.)

Kenai National Wildlife Refuge: There is a mixture of habitats including alpine tundra, boreal forest, muskegs, and coastal wetlands. This refuge is known for its canoe routes, which include more than 40 lakes. It is possible to see nesting Common and Pacific Loons, Red-necked and Horned Grebes, and Trumpeter Swans. Access is via the Sterling Highway, about 120 miles from Anchorage.

Kenai River Flats: In spring this is a good place to see Snow Geese, Greater White-fronted Geese, Sandhill Cranes, and numerous ducks. Viewing is available along Bridge Road near the town of Kenai.

Nancy Lake Recreation Area: This area of lakes, streams, and bogs in a boreal forest is home to nesting loons, grebes, and Ospreys. Access is 31 miles west of Palmer off the George Parks Highway.

Western Alaska

This region is dominated by tundra with a strong marine influence. It includes the immense Yukon-Kuskokwim Delta, one of the most important waterfowl and shorebird nesting areas in North America.

Gambell–St. Lawrence Island: This island is located in the middle of the Bering Sea, where birders come from all over, hoping to add species to their life and North American lists. A number of Asiatic species show up here on a regular basis.

Nome Area: This area is the only place in Alaska where you can step off a commercial jetliner, rent a car, and search for an exciting mix of arctic and Siberian birds. Three well-maintained roads lead from town into a variety of habitats. Possible species include Arctic Loons, Yellow-billed Loons, Black-bellied Plovers, Bristle-thighed Curlews, Wandering Tattlers, Red Knots, Red Phalaropes, Long-tailed Jaegers, Pomarine Jaegers, and Parasitic Jaegers, Slaty-backed Gulls,

Sabine's Gulls, Arctic Warblers, Bluethroats, Gray-cheeked Thrushes, and White Wagtails. See *Birds of the Seward Peninsula, Alaska,* by B. Kessel (University of Alaska Press, Fairbanks, 1989).

Northern Alaska

Bordered by the Arctic Ocean to the north and the Brooks Range to the south, this region consists of treeless Arctic tundra. The polar ice pack covers the marine waters for 8 to 9 months each year and is never far offshore. A productive habitat for nesting birds in summer, in winter the region becomes locked in ice and darkness, and most birds leave. See *Birds of the Beaufort Sea,* by S. R. Johnson and D. R. Herter (BP Exploration Inc., Anchorage, 1989).

Barrow Area: Jutting into the Arctic Ocean, this is the most northerly part of Alaska. Possible sightings may include King, Common, and Steller's Eiders, several shorebird species, all the jaegers, Black Guillemots, Snowy Owls, and Snow Buntings. In fall large numbers of Ross's Gulls migrate past Point Barrow, and spectacular migrations of eiders can be seen in this area. The town of Barrow has daily jet service, lodging, truck rental, and packaged tours.

PHOTOGRAPHING ALASKA'S BIRDS

Boreal Owl, with prey
I set up an infrared beam and electronic flash to let
this owl take its own photo as it flew to the nest.

T hrough the challenge of photography, I have been able to identify birds more easily, have learned more about their habits, and have had fun. Very few birds, however, are easy to photograph. Over the years, I have read every "how-to" book I could find, tried many of the suggested techniques, and stumbled onto a few of my own. Here is what has worked for me.

Equipment and Techniques

Telephoto lenses in the 300 to 400mm category are my favorite. They must be able to focus to at least 8 to 10 feet in order to obtain frame-filling photos of small birds. They must be at least f5.6 to use Kodachrome 64 at 1/500 second on a sunny day, a shutter speed helpful in obtaining sharp images of birds in flight. My favorite lens is the light and compact Nikon 300mm f4.5. I use a 1.4 tele-extender to boost it to 420mm.

I usually carry two camera bodies. One has some automatic features, such as aperture preferred, to respond to changing light conditions in a remote setup (where you are away from the camera). The other is completely mechanical, which is more reliable (there is less to go wrong) and useful as a backup. I find essential both a motor drive that can operate in a continuous mode and one that can be triggered remotely.

I use two tripods, both Bogens. One is light, for packing long distances; the other is medium-heavy for maximum steadiness. The legs on Bogen tripods can be spread far apart for nearly ground-level work. I also use a table tripod. These are perfect for use while lying flat and for photographing ground-nesting birds.

I have sat patiently near a feeder, used a blind, set off cameras remotely, and photographed through a window. Cameras can be triggered remotely by using a long cable or air release (the cheapest), an infrared triggering device ($100 to $200), or a radio-controlled device (the most expensive alternative). Even a few of the completely automatic cameras, the ones without interchangeable lenses, have remote triggering devices, which can enable you to obtain great, frame-filling photos of birds at feeders without using expensive telephoto lenses. Photographs can also be taken through a window. Use a black cloth with a hole for the lens to eliminate reflections.

I have found John Shaw's *The Nature Photographer's Complete Guide to Professional Field Techniques* (Amphoto, 1984) to be the most useful for equipment and some techniques.

Cameras and Inclement Weather

If it is below freezing, and the camera has been set out for some time, I always put it in a small plastic garbage bag and tie a knot in the top before bringing it into a warm room. This causes condensation to form on the inside of the bag rather than on the camera. For remote setups where rain is a possibility, I put a plastic bag over the camera, cut a hole for the lens, and secure it with a lens hood.

Blinds

My favorite blind is homemade, and it consists of a folding lawn chair, aluminum tubing, and camouflage fabric. It's not much larger than a person sitting, it's very comfortable, and it can be easily moved. Avoid types of blinds that require pegs and ropes to hold them in place. Invariably, once you set up, you need to move it a few feet.

Stalking

Very few species can be stalked; birds are just too wary. Some shorebirds can be stalked by lying flat on the ground and inching along commando-style. Many times I have crawled in among shorebirds, taken photographs, and left without disturbing them. A table tripod helps keep the camera out of the mud and is a perfect height for the prone position. For other birds, moving very slowly,

Great Blue Heron on a dock during a snowstorm. I laid down in the middle of the road to get this photo, with a 560mm lens.

stopping whenever they seem nervous, and keeping in full view sometimes works.

Feeding

Any bird that can be attracted to a feeder can be photographed. The trick is to make the scene look natural. A perch placed above the seed for the birds to land on or a moss-covered log with a hidden cavity for the seed are my favorite props. For hummingbirds, I place a flower in a vase near the feeder. Some will always try it out.

Flying Birds

Waiting for birds to come to you sometimes works. Some birds, such as feeding gulls, geese, and Bald Eagles, habitually fly past certain areas. I usually photograph them in flight by using a hand-held camera with a motor drive set

This Chestnut-backed Chickadee was photographed at a feeder, through a closed window, using an electronic flash.

in the continuous mode. To stop camera and bird movement, a general rule of thumb is to use a shutter speed equal to or greater than the length of the lens. The best success, for example, is obtained when using 1/500 second with a 300 to 400mm lens. It is also difficult to focus on flying birds, so when I think the bird is in focus, I fire the camera in bursts of 3 to 5 frames while following the bird. This technique uses more film but increases the probability of obtaining a couple of sharp images.

Nesting Birds

Photographing birds at their nest is the best and sometimes the only way to photograph many species. Unfortunately, it is also the most dangerous for the bird. If you follow a few rules, and if you use certain equipment and

This photograph of a Semipalmated Plover at its nest was triggered from 200 feet away by an infrared device. I used a 50mm lens, and a split-field lens was used to bring the glacier into focus.

techniques, the possibility of harming the eggs or young becomes unlikely, and stress on the parents is much reduced.

As with all nature subjects, the welfare of the bird should always be a higher priority than obtaining the photograph. Try to pick nest sites where you are apt to be the only photographer. A bird may tolerate one or two photo sessions, but visits by several photographers may be too disruptive. For this reason most national parks, including Denali, do not allow photographers near nesting birds. In addition, you must first get a permit from the U. S. Fish and Wildlife Service to photograph eagles at their nest.

If Eggs Are Present: If a bird is disturbed while building a nest, before the clutch is finished, or even during the early days of incubation, it may desert the nest. But as incubation progresses, so does the bird's tolerance of disturbance. The eggs of most birds can tolerate a considerable amount of chilling. This means that keeping a bird away from its nest for short periods of time will not harm the eggs.

If Young Are Present: Studies have shown that newly hatched chicks were much more harmed by low temperature than were eggs at any stage of incubation. When an infant bird hatches, it must be brooded by the parent. This dries it out and helps maintain sufficient warmth in its body. This is very important, as the young bird is born cold-blooded, and it takes a certain amount of time for the youngster to establish its own temperature control, or warm-bloodedness.

If the young are precocial (eyes open, down-covered), as in shorebirds, this time is very short, and the young may leave the nest site as early as a few hours after hatching. In general, if precocial young are not wet but fluffy and dry, and if the weather is warm and dry, it's probably safe to set up for photography.

If the young are altricial (eyes closed, little or no down), as in songbirds, the parents may brood the young most of the time for the first few days after hatching. It's best to wait until altricial young have their eyes open and have developed a good set of down feathers before attempting any photography.

Move about the nest site as quickly as possible. Your equipment should be preassembled as much as possible before you approach the nest site. I have found it best and least disturbing to the parent birds to use a wireless remote control to trigger the camera. Most birds accept a camera by itself rather quickly, and many return to the nest almost immediately after you leave the area. Using this equipment, you simply sit some distance away and watch with binoculars or a spotting scope for the most opportune time to trigger the camera.

Songbirds

Very few species of songbirds will come to feeders. Stalking these small, nervous birds seldom works, and many species build nests that are almost impossible to find. To lure songbirds within photographic distance, the best

This Song Sparrow was attracted close enough to photograph by a recording of its voice.

method I have found is to record their singing and play it back to them. In spring and early summer, male songbirds sing to establish and maintain territories. This territorial behavior is quite strong, and the birds will usually defend their territories from the intruder they assume is nearby when they hear the recording. Usually they are so intent on driving the intruder away that the photographer can stand in the open and expect to obtain photographs from a distance of only 7 to 10 feet.

The welfare of the birds must be considered when using recordings, as constant use may also drive them from their territories. I usually quit after about 1 hour, or if the male's response begins to weaken, or if the female begins chasing the male. As with photographing at nests, it's best to work in areas where you are apt to be the only one using this technique. Playing birdsongs is banned in most national parks, including Denali.

— CHECKLIST —

of Alaska's Birds

This checklist includes all birds found in Alaska based on Gibson's checklist, 1993. Birds that do not occur in Alaska every year are indicated by an asterisk * (these are classed as accidental or casual). Sequence follows the American Ornithologists' Union *Check-list of North American Birds*.

Loons
__ Red-throated Loon
__ Arctic Loon
__ Pacific Loon
__ Common Loon
__ Yellow-billed Loon

Grebes
__ Pied-billed Grebe
__ Horned Grebe
__ Red-necked Grebe
__ Western Grebe

Albatrosses
__ Short-tailed Albatross
__ Black-footed Albatross
__ Laysan Albatross

Fulmars, Petrels, Shearwaters
__ Northern Fulmar
__ Mottled Petrel
__ Cook's Petrel*
__ Sooty Shearwater
__ Short-tailed Shearwater

Storm-Petrels
__ Fork-tailed Storm-Petrel

__ Leach's Storm-Petrel

Pelicans
__ American White Pelican*

Cormorants
__ Double-crested Cormorant
__ Brandt's Cormorant
__ Pelagic Cormorant
__ Red-faced Cormorant

Frigatebirds
__ Magnificent Frigatebird*

Bitterns, Herons
__ American Bittern
__ Yellow Bittern*
__ Great Blue Heron
__ Great Egret*
__ Chinese Egret*
__ Cattle Egret*
__ Green-backed Heron*
__ Black-crowned Night-Heron*

Swans, Geese, Ducks
__ Tundra Swan
__ Whooper Swan

__ Trumpeter Swan
__ Bean Goose
__ Greater White-fronted Goose
__ Snow Goose
__ Ross's Goose*
__ Emperor Goose
__ Brant
__ Canada Goose
__ Wood Duck*
__ Green-winged Teal
__ Baikal Teal*
__ Falcated Teal*
__ American Black Duck*
__ Mallard
__ Spot-billed Duck*
__ Northern Pintail
__ Garganey
__ Blue-winged Teal
__ Cinnamon Teal
__ Northern Shoveler
__ Gadwall
__ Eurasian Wigeon
__ American Wigeon
__ Common Pochard
__ Canvasback
__ Redhead
__ Ring-necked Duck
__ Tufted Duck
__ Greater Scaup
__ Lesser Scaup
__ Common Eider
__ King Eider
__ Spectacled Eider
__ Steller's Eider
__ Harlequin Duck
__ Oldsquaw
__ Black Scoter
__ Surf Scoter
__ White-winged Scoter
__ Common Goldeneye
__ Barrow's Goldeneye
__ Bufflehead
__ Smew

__ Hooded Merganser
__ Common Merganser
__ Red-breasted Merganser
__ Ruddy Duck

American Vultures
__ Turkey Vulture*

Hawks, Eagles, Harriers, Ospreys
__ Osprey
__ Bald Eagle
__ White-tailed Eagle*
__ Steller's Sea-Eagle*
__ Northern Harrier
__ Sharp-shinned Hawk
__ Northern Goshawk
__ Swainson's Hawk
__ Red-tailed Hawk
__ Rough-legged Hawk
__ Golden Eagle

Falcons
__ Eurasian Kestrel*
__ American Kestrel
__ Merlin
__ Northern Hobby*
__ Peregrine Falcon
__ Gyrfalcon

Grouse, Ptarmigans
__ Spruce Grouse
__ Blue Grouse
__ Willow Ptarmigan
__ Rock Ptarmigan
__ White-tailed Ptarmigan
__ Ruffed Grouse
__ Sharp-tailed Grouse

Rails, Gallinules, Coots
__ Virginia Rail*
__ Sora
__ Eurasian Coot*
__ American Coot

Cranes
__ Sandhill Crane
__ Common Crane*

Plovers
__ Black-bellied Plover
__ American Golden-Plover
__ Pacific Golden-Plover
__ Mongolian Plover
__ Snowy Plover*
__ Common Ringed Plover
__ Semipalmated Plover
__ Little Ringed Plover*
__ Killdeer
__ Eurasian Dotterel

Oystercatchers
__ Black Oystercatcher

Stilts, Avocets
__ Black-winged Stilt*
__ American Avocet*

Pratincoles
__ Oriental Pratincole*

Sandpipers
__ Common Greenshank
__ Greater Yellowlegs
__ Lesser Yellowlegs
__ Marsh Sandpiper*
__ Spotted Redshank*
__ Wood Sandpiper
__ Green Sandpiper*
__ Solitary Sandpiper
__ Wandering Tattler
__ Gray-tailed Tattler
__ Common Sandpiper
__ Spotted Sandpiper
__ Terek Sandpiper*
__ Upland Sandpiper
__ Little Curlew*
__ Eskimo Curlew*
__ Whimbrel

__ Bristle-thighed Curlew
__ Far Eastern Curlew*
__ Black-tailed Godwit*
__ Hudsonian Godwit
__ Bar-tailed Godwit
__ Marbled Godwit
__ Ruddy Turnstone
__ Black Turnstone
__ Surfbird
__ Great Knot*
__ Red Knot
__ Sanderling
__ Semipalmated Sandpiper
__ Western Sandpiper
__ Rufous-necked Stint
__ Little Stint*
__ Temminck's Stint*
__ Long-toed Stint
__ Least Sandpiper
__ White-rumped Sandpiper
__ Baird's Sandpiper
__ Pectoral Sandpiper
__ Sharp-tailed Sandpiper
__ Purple Sandpiper*
__ Rock Sandpiper
__ Dunlin
__ Curlew Sandpiper*
__ Stilt Sandpiper
__ Spoonbill Sandpiper*
__ Broad-billed Sandpiper*
__ Buff-breasted Sandpiper
__ Ruff
__ Short-billed Dowitcher
__ Long-billed Dowitcher
__ Jack Snipe*
__ Common Snipe
__ Pin-tailed Snipe*
__ Wilson's Phalarope*
__ Red-necked Phalarope
__ Red Phalarope

Jaegers, Gulls, Terns
__ Pomarine Jaeger
__ Parasitic Jaeger

__ Long-tailed Jaeger
__ South Polar Skua*
__ Franklin's Gull*
__ Common Black-headed Gull
__ Bonaparte's Gull
__ Heermann's Gull*
__ Black-tailed Gull*
__ Mew Gull
__ Ring-billed Gull
__ California Gull
__ Herring Gull
__ Iceland Gull
__ Slaty-backed Gull
__ Lesser Black-backed Gull*
__ Western Gull*
__ Glaucous-winged Gull
__ Glaucous Gull
__ Black-legged Kittiwake
__ Red-legged Kittiwake
__ Ross's Gull
__ Sabine's Gull
__ Ivory Gull
__ Caspian Tern
__ Common Tern
__ Arctic Tern
__ Aleutian Tern
__ White-winged Tern*
__ Black Tern*

Alcids
__ Dovekie
__ Common Murre
__ Thick-billed Murre
__ Black Guillemot
__ Pigeon Guillemot
__ Marbled Murrelet
__ Kittlitz's Murrelet
__ Ancient Murrelet
__ Cassin's Auklet
__ Parakeet Auklet
__ Least Auklet
__ Whiskered Auklet
__ Crested Auklet
__ Rhinoceros Auklet

__ Tufted Puffin
__ Horned Puffin

Pigeons, Doves
__ Rock Dove
__ Band-tailed Pigeon
__ Oriental Turtle-Dove*
__ White-winged Dove*
__ Mourning Dove

Cuckoos
__ Common Cuckoo*
__ Oriental Cuckoo*
__ Yellow-billed Cuckoo*

Typical Owls
__ Oriental Scops-Owl*
__ Western Screech-Owl
__ Great Horned Owl
__ Snowy Owl
__ Northern Hawk Owl
__ Northern Pygmy-Owl
__ Barred Owl
__ Great Gray Owl
__ Long-eared Owl*
__ Short-eared Owl
__ Boreal Owl
__ Northern Saw-whet Owl

Goatsuckers
__ Lesser Nighthawk*
__ Common Nighthawk
__ Whip-poor-will*
__ Jungle Nightjar*

Swifts
__ Black Swift
__ Chimney Swift*
__ Vaux's Swift
__ White-throated Needletail*
__ Common Swift*
__ Fork-tailed Swift*

Hummingbirds
__ Ruby-throated Hummingbird*
__ Anna's Hummingbird
__ Costa's Hummingbird*
__ Rufous Hummingbird

Hoopoes
__ Hoopoe*

Kingfishers
__ Belted Kingfisher

Woodpeckers
__ Eurasian Wryneck*
__ Yellow-bellied Sapsucker*
__ Red-breasted Sapsucker
__ Great Spotted Woodpecker*
__ Downy Woodpecker
__ Hairy Woodpecker
__ Three-toed Woodpecker
__ Black-backed Woodpecker
__ Northern Flicker

Tyrant Flycatchers
__ Olive-sided Flycatcher
__ Western Wood-Pewee
__ Yellow-bellied Flycatcher*
__ Alder Flycatcher
__ Willow Flycatcher*
__ Least Flycatcher
__ Hammond's Flycatcher
__ Dusky Flycatcher*
__ Pacific-slope Flycatcher
__ Eastern Phoebe*
__ Say's Phoebe
__ Great Crested Flycatcher*
__ Tropical Kingbird*
__ Western Kingbird*
__ Eastern Kingbird

Larks
__ Eurasian Skylark
__ Horned Lark

Swallows
__ Purple Martin*
__ Tree Swallow
__ Violet-green Swallow
__ Northern Rough-winged
   Swallow
__ Bank Swallow
__ Cliff Swallow
__ Barn Swallow
__ Common House-Martin*

Jays, Magpies, Crows
__ Gray Jay
__ Steller's Jay
__ Clark's Nutcracker*
__ Black-billed Magpie
__ American Crow
__ Northwestern Crow
__ Common Raven

Chickadees
__ Black-capped Chickadee
__ Mountain Chickadee*
__ Siberian Tit
__ Boreal Chickadee
__ Chestnut-backed Chickadee

Nuthatches
__ Red-breasted Nuthatch

Creepers
__ Brown Creeper

Wrens
__ Winter Wren

Dippers
__ American Dipper

Old World Warblers, Kinglets, Old World Flycatchers, Thrushes
__ Middendorff's Grasshopper-
   Warbler*

__ Lanceolated Warbler*
__ Wood Warbler*
__ Dusky Warbler*
__ Arctic Warbler
__ Golden-crowned Kinglet
__ Ruby-crowned Kinglet
__ Narcissus Flycatcher*
__ Red-breasted Flycatcher*
__ Siberian Flycatcher*
__ Gray-spotted Flycatcher*
__ Asian Brown Flycatcher*
__ Siberian Rubythroat
__ Bluethroat
__ Siberian Blue Robin*
__ Red-flanked Bluetail*
__ Northern Wheatear
__ Stonechat*
__ Mountain Bluebird
__ Townsend's Solitaire
__ Veery*
__ Gray-cheeked Thrush
__ Swainson's Thrush
__ Hermit Thrush
__ Eyebrowed Thrush
__ Dusky Thrush*
__ Fieldfare*
__ American Robin
__ Varied Thrush

Mimic Thrushes
__ Northern Mockingbird*
__ Brown Thrasher*

Accentors
__ Siberian Accentor*

Wagtails, Pipits
__ Yellow Wagtail
__ Gray Wagtail*
__ White Wagtail
__ Black-backed Wagtail
__ Brown Tree-Pipit*
__ Olive Tree-Pipit*
__ Pechora Pipit*

__ Red-throated Pipit
__ American Pipit

Waxwings
__ Bohemian Waxwing
__ Cedar Waxwing

Shrikes
__ Brown-Shrike*
__ Northern Shrike

Starlings
__ European Starling

Vireos
__ Solitary Vireo*
__ Warbling Vireo
__ Philadelphia Vireo*
__ Red-eyed Vireo

Wood Warblers, Tanagers, Sparrows, Buntings, Blackbirds
__ Tennessee Warbler
__ Orange-crowned Warbler
__ Yellow Warbler
__ Magnolia Warbler
__ Cape May Warbler*
__ Yellow-rumped Warbler
__ Townsend's Warbler
__ Black-throated Green Warbler*
__ Prairie Warbler*
__ Palm Warbler*
__ Blackpoll Warbler
__ Black-and-White Warbler*
__ American Redstart
__ Ovenbird*
__ Northern Waterthrush
__ Mourning Warbler*
__ MacGillivray's Warbler
__ Common Yellowthroat
__ Wilson's Warbler
__ Canada Warbler*

___ Scarlet Tanager*
___ Western Tanager
___ Blue Grosbeak*
___ Indigo Bunting*
___ Rufous-sided Towhee*
___ American Tree Sparrow
___ Chipping Sparrow
___ Clay-colored Sparrow*
___ Brewer's Sparrow*
___ Lark Sparrow*
___ Savannah Sparrow
___ Fox Sparrow
___ Song Sparrow
___ Lincoln's Sparrow
___ Swamp Sparrow*
___ White-throated Sparrow*
___ Golden-crowned Sparrow
___ White-crowned Sparrow
___ Harris's Sparrow
___ Dark-eyed Junco
___ Lapland Longspur
___ Smith's Longspur
___ Pine Bunting*
___ Little Bunting*
___ Rustic Bunting
___ Yellow-breasted Bunting*
___ Gray Bunting*
___ Pallas's Reed-Bunting*
___ Common Reed-Bunting*
___ Snow Bunting
___ McKay's Bunting

___ Bobolink*
___ Red-winged Blackbird
___ Western Meadowlark*
___ Yellow-headed Blackbird*
___ Rusty Blackbird
___ Brewer's Blackbird*
___ Common Grackle*
___ Brown-headed Cowbird

Finches
___ Brambling
___ Gray-crowned Rosy-Finch
___ Pine Grosbeak
___ Common Rosefinch*
___ Purple Finch*
___ Cassin's Finch*
___ Red Crossbill
___ White-winged Crossbill
___ Common Redpoll
___ Hoary Redpoll
___ Eurasian Siskin*
___ Pine Siskin
___ American Goldfinch*
___ Oriental Greenfinch*
___ Eurasian Bullfinch*
___ Evening Grosbeak*
___ Hawfinch*

Old World Sparrows
___ House Sparrow*

Armstrong, R. H. *Guide to the Birds of Alaska.* Seattle: Alaska Northwest Books, 1990. Covers identification, habitat, status, and distribution of Alaska's birds. Includes photographs of most species and paintings of some. A handy chart giving the abundance by season for each region of Alaska is included with each species account.

Bellrose, F. C. *Ducks, Geese and Swans of North America.* Harrisburg, PA: Stackpole Books, 1976. My favorite reference on waterfowl. Excellent maps show where each species winters, breeds, and migrates. Good coverage of Alaska.

Bent, A. C. *Life Histories of North American Birds.* U. S. National Museum Bulletins, 1919–1958. Each species account contains observations by different naturalists on the birds' habits and behavior. If you can't find anything interesting elsewhere about a bird, look in Bent.

Ehrlich, P. R., D. S. Dobkin, and D. Wheye. *The Birder's Handbook.* New York: Simon and Schuster, 1988. Loaded with information, a marvelous companion to your field guide. Essays condense the scientific literature into readable, interesting material.

Gabrielson, I. N., and F. C. Lincoln. *The Birds of Alaska.* Harrisburg, PA: The Stackpole Company; and Washington, D.C.: Wildlife Management Institute, 1959. For the habits and behavior of some birds in Alaska, this may be the only source of information.

Gibson, D. D. *Checklist of Alaska Birds.* Fairbanks: University of Alaska Museum, 1993. This complete list of all species that have been identified in Alaska is updated every so often, and is considered the authority on the species found in the state.

Gibson, D. D., and B. Kessel. "Seventy-Four New Avian Taxa Documented in Alaska 1976–1991," in *Condor* 94 (22), 1992. An important scientific publication for anyone interested in the status and distribution of Alaska's birds. The "Literature Cited" section contains numerous other sources of information on Alaska's birds.

Haley, D., ed. *Seabirds of Eastern North Pacific and Arctic Waters*. Seattle: Pacific Search Press, 1984. Written by various ornithologists in an easy-to-understand manner, yet loaded with useful factual material. Outstanding photographs and illustrations.

Kessel, B., and D. D. Gibson. *Status and Distribution of Alaska Birds*. Studies in Avian Biology No. 1. Los Angeles: Cooper Ornithological Society, 1978. Provides information on the status and distribution of Alaska's birds not covered by Gabrielson and Lincoln (1959).

Lincoln, F. C. *Migration of Birds*. Circular 16. U.S. Fish and Wildlife Service, 1979. Condenses an enormous amount of material and helps us understand where most of Alaska's birds come from.

Ogilvie, M. A. *The Winter Birds: Birds of the Arctic*. New York: Praeger Publishers, 1976. A readable account of how birds adapt to life in the Arctic.

Palmer, R. S., ed. *Handbook of North American Birds*. 5 vols. New Haven: Yale University Press, 1962–1988. Each species account is written by an expert on that species. Although loaded with technical information, each account has a concise, accessible section on birds' habits.

Steinhart, P. *Tracks in the Sky*. San Francisco: Chronicle Books, 1987. A book about wetlands, their importance, and their beauty. A "must" for anyone concerned about the future of Alaska's birds. The photography by Tupper Ansel Blake is excellent.

Terres, J. K. *The Audubon Society Encyclopedia of North American Birds*. New York: Alfred A. Knopf, 1980. If I could own only one reference book on birds, this would be my choice. I use this encyclopedia more than any other bird book.

— INDEX —

Numbers in **boldface** refer to photographs.
References to illustrations are printed in *italics*.

Alaska Northwest Books™ is proud to publish another
book in its Alaska Pocket Guide series, designed with the
curious traveler in mind. Ask for more books in this series at your
favorite bookstore, or contact Alaska Northwest Books™.

ALASKA NORTHWEST BOOKS™

An Imprint of Graphic Arts Center Publishing Company
P.O. Box 10306, Portland, OR 97210
800-452-3032